Let the Living Bible Help You

The whole Bible was given us by inspiration from God and is useful to teach us what is true and to make us realize what is wrong in our lives; it straightens us out and helps us do what is right.

It is God's way of making us well prepared at every point, fully equipped to do good to everyone.

2 Timothy 3: 16, 17

Let
The Living Bible
Help You

ALICE ZILLMAN CHAPIN

HARPER & ROW, PUBLISHERS
NEW YORK, EVANSTON,
SAN FRANCISCO, LONDON

To my mother

LET THE LIVING BIBLE HELP YOU. Copyright © 1975 by Alice Zillman Chapin. All rights reserved. Printed in the United States of America. For information address Harper & Row, Publishers, Inc., 10 East 53rd Street, New York, N.Y. 10022. Published simultaneously in Canada by Fitzhenry & Whiteside Limited, Toronto.

FIRST EDITION

ISBN: 0-06-061582-6

LIBRARY OF CONGRESS CATALOG CARD NUMBER: 74-25689

Contents

A Word From the Editor

In this hectic, harried twentieth century, we humans need a quieter for our minds. We need a stabilizer for our inner being. We search for it urgently, but cannot find it in psychiatry, meditation, drugs, or alcohol. Yet this quieter was given to us hundreds of years ago.

We have ignored the Bible, pretended it wasn't there, declared its author dead, burned it, and denied its truths. Now some of us are doing a turnabout. There is a quickening pace toward God. The Bible is becoming increasingly sensed as the place to find the anchor our souls desperately seek.

But where do you look for solutions to daily problems? Where in the Bible can you look for help if you feel sad, angry, lonely, restless, or afraid? If you are considering divorce? If your business has failed? If you are sick or suffering? If an elderly parent wants to live with you? Surely it should not be necessary to consult a middle person, a busy clergyman, to find some reading from God's Word that will give instant help for specific problems!

As a teacher and daily reader of God's Word, I knew the answers were there. I had often been helped by God's promises to me as a follower of His way. I had been restrained, too, by the cautions in the Bible. Yet I could not always locate just the "right verses" to counsel others, to help myself through the hard days, or to praise God on happy days. So I assembled these readings from *The Living Bible*.

Jesus said, "I came that you might have life and have it more abundantly." Not many have found that much sought-after quiet heart in the midst of this fearsome, pressure-cooker world. I have as a follower of Jesus.

Are you searching for such peace? If you have not yet committed your life to Christ as a satisfying way to live in the twentieth century, turn to the back pages of this book to find out how you can. You can't *buy* the promises in God's Word. They aren't for sale. They are *free* to committed Christians.

Alice Zillman Chapin

❧ 1 ❧

When You Feel Afraid, Anxious, Worried

Trust God

ROMANS 8

31 What can we ever say to such wonderful things as these? If God is on our side, who can ever be against us?

PSALM 55

17 I will pray morning, noon, and night, pleading aloud with God; and he will hear and answer.

18 Though the tide of battle runs strongly against me, for so many are fighting me, yet he will rescue me.

22 Give your burdens to the Lord. He will carry them. He will not permit the godly to slip or fall.

PROVERBS 20

24 Since the Lord is directing our steps, why try to understand everything that happens along the way?

PROVERBS 3

4,5 If you want favor with both God and man, and a reputation for good judgment and common sense, then trust the Lord completely; don't ever trust yourself.

I

6 In everything you do, put God first, and he will direct you and crown your efforts with success.

PSALM 124

8 Our help is from the Lord who made heaven and earth.

PSALM 125

1 Those who trust in the Lord are steady as Mount Zion, unmoved by any circumstance.

2 Just as the mountains surround and protect Jerusalem, so the Lord surrounds and protects his people.

You can trust someone who loves you

1 JOHN 4

16 We know how much God loves us because we have felt his love and because we believe him when he tells us that he loves us dearly. God is love, and anyone who lives in love is living with God and God is living in him.

18 We need have no fear of someone who loves us perfectly; his perfect love for us eliminates all dread of what he might do to us. If we are afraid, it is for fear of what he might do to us, and shows that we are not fully convinced that he really loves us.

19 So you see, our love for him comes as a result of his loving us first.

Worry won't add a single moment to your life

MATTHEW 6

25 So my counsel is: Don't worry about *things*—food, drink, and clothes. For you already have life and a body—and they are far more important than what to eat and wear.

26 Look at the birds! They don't worry about what to eat—they don't need to sow or reap or store up food—for your heavenly Father feeds them. And you are far more valuable to him than they are.

27 Will all your worries add a single moment to your life?

28 And why worry about your clothes? Look at the field lilies! They don't worry about theirs.

29 Yet King Solomon in all his glory was not clothed as beautifully as they.

30 And if God cares so wonderfully for flowers that are here today and gone tomorrow, won't he more surely care for you, O men of little faith?

31,32 So don't worry at all about having enough food and clothing. Why be like the heathen? For they take pride in all these things and are deeply concerned about them. But your heavenly Father already knows perfectly well that you need them,

33 And he will give them to you if you give him first place in your life.

34 So don't be anxious about tomorrow. God will take care of your tomorrow too. Live one day at a time.

LUKE 12

22 Then turning to his disciples he said, "Don't worry about whether you have enough food to eat or clothes to wear.

24 Look at the ravens—they don't plant or harvest or have barns to store away their food, and yet they get along all right—for God feeds them. And you are far more valuable to him than any birds!

25 And besides, what's the use of worrying? What good does it do? Will it add a single day to your life? Of course not!

PHILIPPIANS 4

4 Always be full of joy in the Lord; I say it again, rejoice!

6 Don't worry about anything; instead, pray about everything; tell God your needs and don't forget to thank him for his answers.

7 If you do this you will experience God's peace, which is far more wonderful than the human mind can understand. His peace will keep your thoughts and your hearts quiet and at rest as you trust in Christ Jesus.

God provides sure safety

PSALM 18

2 The Lord is my fort where I can enter and be safe; no one can follow me in and slay me. He is a rugged mountain where I hide; he is my Savior, a rock where none can reach me, and a tower of safety. He is my shield. He is like the strong horn of a mighty fighting bull.

30 What a God he is! How perfect in every way! All his promises prove true. He is a shield for everyone who hides behind him.

32 He fills me with strength and protects me wherever I go.

33 He gives me the surefootedness of a mountain goat upon the crags. He leads me safely along the top of the cliffs.

35 You have given me your salvation as my shield. Your right hand, O Lord, supports me; your gentleness has made me great.

36 You have made wide steps beneath my feet so that I need never slip.

PSALM 121

1 Shall I look to the mountain gods for help?

2 No! My help is from Jehovah who made the mountains! And the heavens too!

3,4 He will never let me stumble, slip or fall. For he is always watching, never sleeping.

5 Jehovah himself is caring for you! He is your defender.

6 He protects you day and night.

ISAIAH 41

10 Fear not, for I am with you. Do not be dismayed. I am your God. I will strengthen you; I will help you; I will uphold you with my victorious right hand.

13 I am holding you by your right hand—I, the Lord your God—and I say to you, Don't be afraid; I am here to help you.

LUKE 6

47,48 But all those who come and listen and obey me are like a man who builds a house on a strong foundation laid upon the underlying rock. When the floodwaters rise and break against the house, it stands firm, for it is strongly built.

JEREMIAH 1

17 Get up and dress and go out and tell them whatever I tell you to say. Don't be afraid of them, or else I will make a fool of you in front of them.

18 For see, today I have made you impervious to their attacks. They cannot harm you. You are strong like a fortified city that cannot be captured, like an iron pillar and heavy gates of brass. All the kings of Judah and its officers and priests and people will not be able to prevail against you.

19 "They will try, but they will fail. For I am with you," says the Lord. "I will deliver you."

The Lord is my helper

HEBREWS 13

6b . . . We can say without any doubt or fear, "The Lord is my Helper and I am not afraid of anything that mere man can do to me."

8 Jesus Christ is the same yesterday, today, and forever.

PSALM 23

1 Because the Lord is my Shepherd, I have everything I need!
2,3 He lets me rest in the meadow grass and leads me beside the quiet streams. He restores my failing health. He helps me do what honors him the most.

4 Even when walking through the dark valley of death I will not be afraid, for you are close beside me, guarding, guiding all the way.

5 You provide delicious food for me in the presence of my enemies. You have welcomed me as your guest; blessings overflow!

6 Your goodness and unfailing kindness shall be with me all of my life, and afterwards I will live with you forever in your home.

PSALM 33

13,14,15 The Lord gazes down upon mankind from heaven where he lives. He has made their hearts and closely watches everything they do.

18,19 But the eyes of the Lord are watching over those who fear him, who rely upon his steady love. He will keep them from death even in times of famine!

20 We depend upon the Lord alone to save us. Only he can help us; he protects us like a shield.

21 No wonder we are happy in the Lord! For we are trusting him. We trust his holy name.

22 Yes, Lord, let your constant love surround us, for our hopes are in you alone.

This is the kind of God we have available to help

MARK 4

35 As evening fell, Jesus said to his disciples, "Let's cross to the other side of the lake."

36 So they took him just as he was and started out, leaving the crowds behind (though other boats followed).

37 But soon a terrible storm arose. High waves began to break into the boat until it was nearly full of water and about to sink.

38 Jesus was asleep at the back of the boat with his head on a cushion. Frantically they wakened him, shouting, "Teacher, don't you even care that we are all about to drown?"

39 Then he rebuked the wind and said to the sea, "Quiet down!" And the wind fell, and there was a great calm!

40 And he asked them, "Why were you so fearful? Don't you even yet have confidence in me?"

41 And they were filled with awe and said among themselves, "Who is this man, that even the winds and seas obey him?"

The Lord is on your side; then praise Him

PSALM 27

1 The Lord is my light and my salvation; whom shall I fear?

2 When evil men come to destroy me, they will stumble and fall!

3 Yes, though a mighty army marches against me, my heart shall know no fear! I am confident that God will save me.

13 I am expecting the Lord to rescue me again, so that once again I will see his goodness to me here in the land of the living.

14 Don't be impatient. Wait for the Lord, and he will come and save you! Be brave, stouthearted and courageous. Yes, wait and he will help you.

PSALM 59

9 O God my Strength! I will sing your praises, for you are my place of safety.

10 My God is changeless in his love for me and he will come and help me...

16 ... I will sing each morning about your power and mercy. For you have been my high tower of refuge, a place of safety in the day of my distress.

7

17 O my Strength, to you I sing my praises; for you are my high tower of safety, my God of mercy.

PSALM 56

3,4 But when I am afraid, I will put my confidence in you. Yes, I will trust the promises of God. And since I am trusting him, what can mere man do to me?

8 You have seen me tossing and turning through the night. You have collected all my tears and preserved them in your bottle! You have recorded every one in your book.

9 The very day I call for help, the tide of battle turns. My enemies flee! This one thing I *know: God is for me!*

10,11 I am trusting God—oh, praise his promises! I am not afraid of anything mere man can do to me! Yes, praise his promises.

12 I will surely do what I have promised, Lord, and thank you for your help.

PSALM 118

1 Oh, thank the Lord, for he's so good! His lovingkindness is forever.

5 In my distress I prayed to the Lord and he answered me and rescued me.

6 He is for me! How can I be afraid? What can mere man do to me?

7 The Lord is on my side, he will help me. Let those who hate me beware.

8 It is better to trust the Lord than to put confidence in men.

9 It is better to take refuge in him than in the mightiest king!

Getting your priorities straight will dispel worry

LUKE 10

38 As Jesus and the disciples continued on their way to Jerusalem they came to a village where a woman named Martha welcomed them into her home.

39 Her sister Mary sat on the floor, listening to Jesus as he talked.

40 But Martha was the jittery type, and was worrying over the big dinner she was preparing. She came to Jesus and said, "Sir, doesn't it seem unfair to you that my sister just sits here while I do all the work? Tell her to come and help me."

41 But the Lord said to her, "Martha, dear friend, you are so upset over all these details!

42 There is really only one thing worth being concerned about. Mary has discovered it—and I won't take it away from her!"

~ 2 ~

When You Are Alone, Lonesome

God is your friend

PSALM 54

4 But God is my helper. He is a friend of mine!

PSALM 14

5b ... For God is with those who love him.

REVELATION 3

20 Look! I have been standing at the door and I am constantly knocking. If anyone hears me calling him and opens the door, I will come in and fellowship with him and he with me.

MATTHEW 10

29 Not one sparrow (What do they cost? Two for a penny?) can fall to the ground without your Father knowing it.

30 And the very hairs of your head are all numbered.

31 So don't worry! You are more valuable to him than many sparrows.

JOSHUA 1

9 Yes, be bold and strong! Banish fear and doubt! For remember, the Lord your God is with you wherever you go.

EPHESIANS 3

12 Now we can come fearlessly right into God's presence, assured of his glad welcome when we come with Christ and trust in him.

EPHESIANS 2

12b . . . You were lost, without God, without hope.

13 But now you belong to Christ Jesus, and though you once were far away from God, now you have been brought very near to him because of what Jesus Christ has done for you with his blood.

18 Now all of us, whether Jews or Gentiles, may come to God the Father with the Holy Spirit's help because of what Christ has done for us.

19 Now you are no longer strangers to God and foreigners to heaven, but you are members of God's very own family, citizens of God's country, and you belong in God's household with every other Christian.

21 We who believe are carefully joined together with Christ as parts of a beautiful, constantly growing temple for God.

22 And you also are joined with him and with each other by the Spirit, and are part of this dwelling place of God.

1 PETER 1

2 Dear friends, God the Father chose you long ago and knew you would become his children.

You are God's child

ROMANS 8

14 For all who are led by the Spirit of God are sons of God.

15 And so we should not be like cringing, fearful slaves, but we should behave like God's very own children, adopted into the bosom of his family, and calling to him, "Father, Father."

16 For his Holy Spirit speaks to us deep in our hearts, and tells us that we really are God's children.

JOHN 14

15,16 If you love me, obey me; and I will ask the Father and he will give you another Comforter, and he will never leave you.

17 He is the Holy Spirit, the Spirit who leads into all truth. The world at large cannot receive him, for it isn't looking for him and doesn't recognize him. But you do, for he lives with you now and some day shall be in you.

18 No, I will not abandon you or leave you as orphans in the storm—I will come to you.

God loves you

JOHN 16

27 For the Father himself loves you dearly because you love me and believe that I came from the Father.

COLOSSIANS 1

20 It was through what his Son did that God cleared a path for everything to come to him—all things in heaven and on earth—for Christ's death on the cross has made peace with God for all by his blood.

21 This includes you who were once so far away from God. You were his enemies and hated him and were separated from him by your evil thoughts and actions, yet now he has brought you back as his friends.

22 He has done this through the death on the cross of his own human body, and now as a result Christ has brought you into the very presence of God, and you are standing there before him with nothing left against you—nothing left that he could even chide you for. . .

EPHESIANS 3

17 And I pray that Christ will be more and more at home in your hearts, living within you as you trust in him. May your roots go down deep into the soil of God's marvelous love;

18,19 And may you be able to feel and understand, as all God's children should, how long, how wide, how deep, and how high his love really is; and to experience this love for yourselves, though it is so great that you will never see the end of it or fully know or understand it. And so at last you will be filled up with God himself.

JOHN 3

15 So that anyone who believes in me will have eternal life.

16 For God loved the world so much that he gave his only Son so that anyone who believes in him shall not perish but have eternal life.

1 CORINTHIANS 2

9 That is what is meant by the Scriptures which say that no mere man has ever seen, heard or even imagined what wonderful things God has ready for those who love the Lord.

ROMANS 8

35 Who then can ever keep Christ's love from us? When we have trouble or calamity, when we are hunted down or destroyed, is it because he doesn't love us anymore? And if we are hungry, or penniless, or in danger, or threatened with death, has God deserted us?

36 No, for the Scriptures tell us that for his sake we must be ready to face death at every moment of the day—we are like sheep awaiting slaughter;

37 But despite all this, overwhelming victory is ours through Christ who loved us enough to die for us.

38 For I am convinced that nothing can ever separate us from his love. Death can't, and life can't. The angels won't, and all the powers of hell itself cannot keep God's love away. Our fears for today, our worries about tomorrow,

39 Or where we are—high above the sky, or in the deepest ocean—nothing will ever be able to separate us from the love of God demonstrated by our Lord Jesus Christ when he died for us.

God is interested in you

1 PETER 5

7 Let him have all your worries and cares, for he is always thinking about you and watching everything that concerns you.

PSALM 32

8 I will instruct you (says the Lord) and guide you along the best pathway for your life; I will advise you and watch your progress.

EPHESIANS 1

4 Long ago, even before he made the world, God chose us to be his very own, through what Christ would do for us; he decided then to make us holy in his eyes, without a single fault—we who stand before him covered with his love.

5 His unchanging plan has always been to adopt us into his own family by sending Jesus Christ to die for us. And he did this because he wanted to!

HEBREWS 4

13 He knows about everyone, everywhere. Everything about us is bare and wide open to the all-seeing eyes of our living God.

God protects you

PSALM 32

7 You are my hiding place from every storm of life; you even keep me from getting into trouble! You surround me with songs of victory.

PSALM 91

1 We live within the shadow of the Almighty, sheltered by the God who is above all gods.

2 This I declare, that he alone is my refuge, my place of safety; he is my God, and I am trusting him.

❦ 3 ❦

When You Are Blue, Discouraged, Depressed

Others have felt the same way before

PSALM 42

1 As the deer pants for water, so I long for you, O God.

2 I thirst for God, the living God. Where can I find him to come and stand before him?

3 Day and night I weep for his help, and all the while my enemies taunt me. "Where is this God of yours?" they scoff.

7 All your waves and billows have gone over me, and floods of sorrow pour upon me like a thundering cataract.

8 Yet day by day the Lord also pours out his steadfast love upon me, and through the night I sing his songs and pray to God who gives me life.

9 "O God my Rock," I cry, "why have you forsaken me? Why must I suffer these attacks from my enemies?"

10 Their taunts pierce me like a fatal wound; again and again they scoff, "Where is that God of yours?"

11 But O my soul, don't be discouraged. Don't be upset. Expect God to act! For I know that I shall again have plenty of reason to praise him for all that he will do. He is my help! He is my God!

PSALM 31

2 Answer quickly when I cry to you; bend low and hear my whispered plea. Be for me a great Rock of safety from my foes.

3 Yes, you are my Rock and my fortress; honor your name by leading me out of this peril.

5,6 Into your hand I commit my spirit. . .

9,10 O Lord, have mercy on me in my anguish. My eyes are red from weeping; my health is broken from sorrow. I am pining away with grief; my years are shortened, drained away because of sadness. My sins have sapped my strength; I stoop with sorrow and with shame.

12 I am forgotten like a dead man, like a broken and discarded pot.

19 Oh, how great is your goodness to those who publicly declare that you will rescue them. For you have stored up great blessings for those who trust and reverence you.

20 Hide your loved ones in the shelter of your presence, safe beneath your hand, safe from all conspiring men.

21 Blessed is the Lord, for he has shown me that his never-failing love protects me like the walls of a fort!

PSALM 102

1 Lord, hear my prayer! Listen to my plea!

2 Don't turn away from me in this time of my distress. Bend down your ear and give me speedy answers,

3,4 for my days disappear like smoke. My health is broken and my heart is sick; it is trampled like grass and is withered. My food is tasteless, and I have lost my appetite.

5 I am reduced to skin and bones because of all my groaning and despair.

6 I am like a vulture in a far-off wilderness, or like an owl alone in the desert.

7 I lie awake, lonely as a solitary sparrow on the roof.

There is hope

1 PETER 5

7 Let him have all your worries and cares, for he is always thinking about you and watching everything that concerns you.

8 Be careful—watch out for attacks from Satan, your great enemy. He prowls around like a hungry, roaring lion, looking for some victim to tear apart.

9 Stand firm when he attacks. Trust the Lord; and remember that other Christians all around the world are going through these sufferings too.

10 After you have suffered a little while, our God, who is full of kindness through Christ, will give you his eternal glory. He personally will come and pick you up, and set you firmly in place, and make you stronger than ever.

11 To him be all power over all things, forever and ever. Amen.

MATTHEW 11

28 Come to me and I will give you rest—all of you who work so hard beneath a heavy yoke.

29,30 Wear my yoke—for it fits perfectly—and let me teach you; for I am gentle and humble, and you shall find rest for your souls; for I give you only light burdens.

ROMANS 8

28 And we know that all that happens to us is working for our good if we love God and are fitting into his plans.

ISAIAH 43

2 When you go through deep waters and great trouble, I will be with you. When you go through rivers of difficulty, you will not drown! When you walk through the fire of oppression, you will not be burned up—the flames will not consume you.

3 For I am the Lord your God, your Savior, the Holy One of Israel.

2 CORINTHIANS 1

3,4 What a wonderful God we have—he is the Father of our Lord Jesus Christ, the source of every mercy, and the one who so wonderfully comforts and strengthens us in our hardships and trials. And why does he do this? So that when others are troubled, needing our sympathy and encouragement, we can pass on to them this same help and comfort God has given us.

5 You can be sure that the more we undergo sufferings for Christ, the more he will shower us with his comfort and encouragement.

1 CORINTHIANS 2

9 That is what is meant by the Scriptures which say that no mere man has ever seen, heard or even imagined what wonderful things God has ready for those who love the Lord.

Praising God is the cure for depression

PSALM 147

17 He hurls the hail upon the earth. Who can stand before his freezing cold?

18 But then he calls for warmer weather, and the spring winds blow and all the river ice is broken.

20b . . . Hallelujah! Yes, praise the Lord!

PHILIPPIANS 4

4 Always be full of joy in the Lord; I say it again, rejoice!

6 Don't worry about anything; instead, pray about everything; tell God your needs and don't forget to thank him for his answers.

7 If you do this you will experience God's peace, which is far more wonderful than the human mind can understand. His peace

will keep your thoughts and your hearts quiet and at rest as you trust in Christ Jesus.

God hears our cries for help

PSALM 34

17 Yes, the Lord hears the good man when he calls to him for help, and saves him out of all his troubles.

18 The Lord is close to those whose hearts are breaking; he rescues those who are humbly sorry for their sins.

19 The good man does not escape all troubles—he has them too. But the Lord helps him in each and every one.

PSALM 40

1 I waited patiently for God to help me; then he listened and heard my cry.

2 He lifted me out of the pit of despair, out from the bog and the mire, and set my feet on a hard, firm path and steadied me as I walked along.

3 He has given me a new song to sing, of praises to our God. Now many will hear of the glorious things he did for me, and stand in awe before the Lord, and put their trust in him.

JOHN 14

18 No, I will not abandon you or leave you as orphans in the storm—I will come to you.

ISAIAH 49

13 Sing for joy, O heavens; shout, O earth. Break forth with song, O mountains, for the Lord has comforted his people, and will have compassion upon them in their sorrow.

14 Yet they say, "My Lord deserted us; he has forgotten us."

15 Never! Can a mother forget her little child and not have love for her own son? Yet even if that should be, I will not forget you.

Don't look back

PHILIPPIANS 3

13 No, dear brothers, I am still not all I should be but I am bringing all my energies to bear on this one thing: Forgetting the past and looking forward to what lies ahead,

14 I strain to reach the end of the race and receive the prize for which God is calling us up to heaven because of what Christ Jesus did for us.

~4~

When You Are Bored

Why boredom comes

PROVERBS 14

14 The backslider gets bored with himself; the godly man's life is exciting.

Consolation in boredom

ECCLESIASTES 3

1 There is a right time for everything:
2 A time to be born, a time to die;
  A time to plant;
  A time to harvest;
3 A time to kill;
  A time to heal;
  A time to destroy;
  A time to rebuild;
4 A time to cry;
  A time to laugh;
  A time to grieve;
  A time to dance;
5 A time for scattering stones;
  A time for gathering stones;
  A time to hug;

A time not to hug;
6 A time to find;
A time to lose;
A time for keeping;
A time for throwing away;
7 A time to tear;
A time to repair;
A time to be quiet;
A time to speak up;
8 A time for loving;
A time for hating;
A time for war;
A time for peace.

GENESIS 1

1 When God began creating the heavens and the earth,

2 the earth was at first a shapeless, chaotic mass, with the Spirit of God brooding over the dark vapors.

3 Then God said, "Let there be light." And light appeared.

4,5 And God was pleased with it, and divided the light from the darkness. So he let it shine for awhile, and then there was darkness again. He called the light "daytime," and the darkness "nighttime." Together they formed the first day.

6 And God said, "Let the vapors separate to form the sky above and the oceans below."

7,8 So God made the sky, dividing the vapor above from the water below. This all happened on the second day.

9,10 Then God said, "Let the water beneath the sky be gathered into oceans so that the dry land will emerge." And so it was. Then God named the dry land "earth," and the water "seas." And God was pleased.

11,12 And he said, "Let the earth burst forth with every sort of grass and seed-bearing plant, and fruit trees with seeds inside the fruit, so that these seeds will produce the kinds of plants and fruits they came from." And so it was, and God was pleased.

13 This all occurred on the third day.

14,15 Then God said, "Let there be bright lights in the sky to give light to the earth and to identify the day and the night; they shall bring about the seasons on the earth, and mark the days and years." And so it was.

16 For God made two huge lights, the sun and moon, to shine down upon the earth—the larger one, the sun, to preside over the day and the smaller one, the moon, to preside through the night; he also made the stars.

17 And God set them in the sky to light the earth,

18 And to preside over the day and night, and to divide the light from the darkness. And God was pleased.

19 This all happened on the fourth day.

20 Then God said, "Let the waters teem with fish and other life, and let the skies be filled with birds of every kind."

21,22 So God created great sea creatures, and every sort of fish and every kind of bird. And God looked at them with pleasure, and blessed them all. "Multiply and stock the oceans," he told them, and to the birds he said, "Let your numbers increase. Fill the earth!"

23 That ended the fifth day.

24 And God said, "Let the earth bring forth every kind of animal —cattle and reptiles and wildlife of every kind." And so it was.

25 God made all sorts of wild animals and cattle and reptiles. And God was pleased with what he had done.

26 Then God said, "Let us make a man—someone like ourselves, to be the master of all life upon the earth and in the skies and in the seas."

27 So God made man like his Maker.
    Like God did God make man;
    Man and maid did he make them.

28 And God blessed them and told them, "Multiply and fill the earth and subdue it; you are masters of the fish and birds and all the animals.

29 And look! I have given you the seed-bearing plants throughout the earth, and all the fruit trees for your food.

30 And I've given all the grass and plants to the animals and birds for their food."

31 Then God looked over all that he had made, and it was excellent in every way. This ended the sixth day.

GENESIS 2

18 And the Lord God said, "It isn't good for man to be alone; I will make a companion for him, a helper suited to his needs."

19,20 So the Lord God formed from the soil every kind of animal and bird, and brought them to the man to see what he would call them; and whatever he called them, that was their name. But still there was no proper helper for the man.

21 Then the Lord God caused the man to fall into a deep sleep, and took one of his ribs and closed up the place from which he had removed it,

22 And made the rib into a woman, and brought her to the man.

23 "This is it!" Adam exclaimed. "She is part of my own bone and flesh! Her name is 'woman' because she was taken out of a man."

24 This explains why a man leaves his father and mother and is joined to his wife in such a way that the two become one person.

25 Now although the man and his wife were both naked, neither of them was embarrassed or ashamed.

With a God like this, how can we be bored?

PSALM 104

1 I bless the Lord: O Lord my God, how great you are! You are robed with honor and with majesty and light! You stretched out the starry curtain of the heavens,

3 And hollowed out the surface of the earth to form the seas. The clouds are his chariots. He rides upon the wings of the wind.

4 The angels are his messengers—his servants of fire!

5 You bound the world together so that it would never fall apart.

6 You clothed the earth with floods of waters covering up the mountains.

7,8 You spoke, and at the sound of your shout the water collected into its vast ocean beds, and mountains rose and valleys sank to the levels you decreed.

9 And then you set a boundary for the seas, so that they would never again cover the earth.

10 He placed springs in the valleys, and streams that gush from the mountains.

11 They give water for all the animals to drink. There the wild donkeys quench their thirst,

12 And the birds nest beside the streams and sing among the branches of the trees.

13 He sends rain upon the mountains and fills the earth with fruit.

14 The tender grass grows up at his command to feed the cattle, and there are fruit trees, vegetables and grain for man to cultivate,

15 And wine to make him glad, and olive oil as lotion for his skin, and bread to give him strength.

16 The Lord planted the cedars of Lebanon. They are tall and flourishing.

17 There the birds make their nests, the storks in the firs.

18 High in the mountains are pastures for the wild goats, and rock-badgers burrow in among the rocks and find protection there.

19 He assigned the moon to mark the months, and the sun to mark the days.

20 He sends the night and darkness, when all the forest folk come out.

21 Then the young lions roar for their food, but they are dependent on the Lord.

22 At dawn they slink back into their dens to rest,

23 And men go off to work until the evening shadows fall again.

24 O Lord, what a variety you have made! And in wisdom you have made them all! The earth is full of your riches.

25 There before me lies the mighty ocean, teeming with life of every kind, both great and small.

26 And look! See the ships! And over there, the whale you made to play in the sea.

27 Every one of these depends on you to give them daily food.

28 You supply it, and they gather it. You open wide your hand to feed them and they are satisfied with all your bountiful provision.

29 But if you turn away from them, then all is lost. And when you gather up their breath, they die and turn again to dust.

30 Then you send your Spirit, and new life is born to replenish all the living of the earth.

31 Praise God forever! How he must rejoice in all his work!

32 The earth trembles at his glance; the mountains burst into flame at his touch.

33 I will sing to the Lord as long as I live. I will praise God to my last breath!

34 May he be pleased by all these thoughts about him, for he is the source of all my joy.

35 Let all sinners perish—all who refuse to praise him. But I will praise him. Hallelujah!

JOB 38

1 Then the Lord *answered Job from the whirlwind:*

2 "Why are you using your ignorance to deny my providence?

3 Now get ready to fight, for I am going to demand some answers from you, and you must reply.

4 Where were you when I laid the foundations of the earth? Tell me, if you know so much.

5 Do you know how its dimensions were determined, and who did the surveying?

6,7 What supports its foundations, and who laid its cornerstone, as the morning stars sang together and all the angels shouted for joy?

8,9 Who decreed the boundaries of the seas when they gushed

from the depths? Who clothed them with clouds and thick darkness,

10 And barred them by limiting their shores,

11 And said, "Thus far and no farther shall you come, and here shall your proud waves stop!"?

12 Have you ever once commanded the morning to appear, and caused the dawn to rise in the east?

13 Have you ever told the daylight to spread to the ends of the earth, to end the night's wickedness?

14 Have you ever robed the dawn in red,

15 And disturbed the haunts of wicked men and stopped the arm raised to strike?

16 Have you explored the springs from which the seas come, or walked in the sources of their depths?

17,18 Has the location of the gates of Death been revealed to you? Do you realize the extent of the earth? Tell me about it if you know!

19 Where does the light come from, and how do you get there? Or tell me about the darkness. Where does it come from?

20 Can you find its boundaries, or go to its source?

21 But of course you know all this! For you were born before it was all created, and you are so very experienced!

22,23 Have you visited the treasuries of the snow, or seen where hail is made and stored? For I have reserved it for the time when I will need it in war.

24 Where is the path to the distribution point of light? Where is the home of the east wind?

25-27 Who dug the valleys for the torrents of rain? Who laid out the path for the lightning, causing the rain to fall upon the barren deserts, so that the parched and barren ground is satisfied with water, and tender grass springs up?

28 Has the rain a father? Where does dew come from?

29 Who is the mother of the ice and frost?

30 For the water changes and turns to ice, as hard as rock.

31 Can you hold back the stars? Can you restrain Orion or Pleiades?

32 Can you ensure the proper sequence of the seasons, or guide the constellation of the Bear with her satellites across the heavens?

33 Do you know the laws of the universe and how the heavens influence the earth?

34 Can you shout to the clouds and make it rain?

35 Can you make lightning appear and cause it to strike as you direct it?

36 Who gives intuition and instinct?

37,38 Who is wise enough to number all the clouds? Who can tilt the water jars of heaven, when everything is dust and clods?

39,40 Can you stalk prey like a lioness, to satisfy the young lions' appetites as they lie in their dens, or lie in wait in the jungle?

41 Who provides for the ravens when their young cry out to God as they try to struggle up from their nest in hunger?

JOB 39

1 Do you know how mountain goats give birth? Have you ever seen them giving birth to their young?

2,3 Do you know how many months of pregnancy they have before they bow themselves to give birth to their young, and carry their burden no longer?

4 Their young grow up in the open field, then leave their parents and return to them no more.

5 Who makes the wild donkeys wild?

6 I have placed them in the wilderness and given them salt plains to live in.

7 For they hate the noise of the city and want no drivers shouting at them!

8 The mountain ranges are their pastureland; there they search for every blade of grass.

9 Will the wild ox be your happy servant? Will he stay beside your feeding crib?

10 Can you use a wild ox to plow with? Will he pull the harrow for you?

11 Because he is so strong, will you trust him? Will you let him decide where to work?

12 Can you send him out to bring in the grain from the threshing-floor?

19 Have you given the horse strength, or clothed his neck with a quivering mane?

20 Have you made him able to leap forward like a locust? His majestic snorting is something to hear!

26 Do you know how a hawk soars and spreads her wings to the south?

27 Is it at your command that the eagle rises high upon the cliffs to make her nest?

28 She lives upon the cliffs, making her home in her mountain fortress.

29 From there she spies her prey, from a very great distance.

Trust and praise as solutions to boredom

PSALM 34

1 I will praise the Lord no matter what happens. I will constantly speak of his glories and grace.

PSALM 50

14,15 What I want from you is your true thanks; I want your promises fulfilled. *I want you to trust me in your times of trouble, so I can rescue you, and you can give me glory.*

Reverence as a solution to boredom

PSALM 86

11 Tell me where you want me to go and I will go there. May every fiber of my being unite in reverence to your name.

PSALM 34

7 For the Angel of the Lord guards and rescues all who reverence him.

8 Oh, put God to the test and see how kind he is! See for yourself the way his mercies shower down on all who trust in him.

9 If you belong to the Lord, reverence him; for everyne who does this has everything he needs.

10 Even strong young lions sometmes go hungry, but those of us who reverence the Lord will never lack any good thing.

11 Sons and daughters, come and listen and let me teach you the importance of trusting and fearing the Lord.

PSALM 17

15 But as for me, my contentment is not in wealth but in seeing you and knowing all is well between us. And when I awake in heaven, I will be fully satisfied, for I will see you face to face.

PSALM 103

1 I bless the holy name of God with all my heart.

2 Yes, I will bless the Lord and not forget the glorious things he does for me.

3 He forgives all my sins. He heals me.

4 He ransoms me from hell. He surrounds me with lovingkindness and tender mercies.

5 He fills my life with good things! My youth is renewed like the eagle's!

6 He gives justice to all who are treated unfairly.

7 He revealed his will and nature to Moses and the people of Israel.

8 He is merciful and tender toward those who don't deserve it; he is slow to get angry and full of kindness and love.

9 He never bears a grudge, nor remains angry forever.

10 He has not punished us as we deserve for all our sins,

11 For his mercy toward those who fear and honor him is as great as the height of the heavens above the earth.

12 He has removed our sins as far away from us as the east is from the west.

13 He is like a father to us, tender and sympathetic to those who reverence him.

14 For he knows we are but dust,

15 And that our days are few and brief, like grass, like flowers,

16 Blown by the wind and gone forever.

17,18 But the lovingkindness of the Lord is from everlasting to everlasting, to those who reverence him; his salvation is to children's children of those who are faithful to his covenant and remember to obey him!

19 The Lord has made the heavens his throne; from there he rules over everything there is.

20 Bless the Lord, you mighty angels of his who carry out his orders, listening for each of his commands.

21 Yes, bless the Lord, you armies of his angels who serve him constantly.

22 Let everything everywhere bless the Lord. And how I bless him too!

Obedience and service as solutions to boredom

PSALM 40

6 It isn't sacrifices and offerings which you really want from your people. Burnt animals bring no special joy to your heart. But you have accepted the offer of my lifelong service.

7 Then I said, "See, I have come, just as all the prophets foretold.

8 And I delight to do your will, my God, for your law is written upon my heart!"

PSALM 22

28 For the Lord is King and rules the nations.

29 Both proud and humble together, all who are mortal—born to die—shall worship him.

30 Our children too shall serve him, for they shall hear from us about the wonders of the Lord;

31 Generations yet unborn shall hear of all the miracles he did for us.

5

When You Can't Get Along With Others

The need to learn to get along with other people

PSALM 133

1 How wonderful it is, how pleasant, when brothers live in harmony!

2 For harmony is as precious as the fragrant anointing oil that was poured over Aaron's head, and ran down onto his beard, and onto the border of his robe.

3 Harmony is as refeshing as the dew on Mount Hermon, on the mountains of Israel.

PROVERBS 29

25 Fear of man is a dangerous trap, but to trust in God means safety.

2 TIMOTHY 1

7 For the Holy Spirit, God's gift, does not want you to be afraid of people, but to be wise and strong, and to love them and enjoy being with them.

Helps and hints for getting along better with people

2 PETER 1

5b . . . For then you must learn to know God better and discover what He wants you to do.

6 Next, learn to put aside your own desires so that you will become patient and godly, gladly letting God have His way with you.

7 This will make possible the next step, which is for you to enjoy other people and to like them, and finally you will grow to love them deeply.

8 The more you go on in this way, the more you will grow strong spiritually and become fruitful and useful to our Lord Jesus Christ.

PROVERBS 16

6 Iniquity is atoned for by mercy and truth; evil is avoided by reverence for God.

7 When a man is trying to please God, God makes even his worst enemies to be at peace with him.

PROVERBS 17

9 Love forgets mistakes; nagging about them parts the best of friends.

22 A cheerful heart does good like medicine, but a broken spirit makes one sick.

ROMANS 12

18 Don't quarrel with anyone. Be at peace with everyone, just as much as possible.

19 Dear friends, never avenge yourselves. Leave that to God, for he has said that he will repay those who deserve it. [Don't take the law into your own hands.]

20 Instead, feed your enemy if he is hungry. If he is thirsty give him something to drink and you will be "heaping coals of fire on

his head." In other words, he will feel ashamed of himself for what he has done to you.

21 Don't let evil get the upper hand but conquer evil by doing good.

1 CORINTHIANS 13

1 If I had the gift of being able to speak in other languages without learning them, and could speak in every language there is in all of heaven and earth, but didn't love others, I would only be making noise.

2 If I had the gift of prophecy and knew all about what is going to happen in the future, knew everything about *everything*, but didn't love others, what good would it do? Even if I had the gift of faith so that I could speak to a mountain and make it move, I would still be worth nothing at all without love.

3 If I gave everything I have to poor people, and if I were burned alive for preaching the Gospel but didn't love others, it would be of no value whatever.

4 Love is very patient and kind, never jealous or envious, never boastful or proud,

5 Never haughty or selfish or rude. Love does not demand its own way. It is not irritable or touchy. It does not hold grudges and will hardly even notice when others do it wrong.

6 It is never glad about injustice, but rejoices whenever truth wins out.

7 If you love someone you will be loyal to him no matter what the cost. You will always believe in him, always expect the best of him, and always stand your ground in defending him.

13 There are three things that remain—faith, hope, and love—and the greatest of these is love.

PROVERBS 29

1 The man who is often reproved but refuses to accept criticism will suddenly be broken and never have another chance.

5,6 Flattery is a trap; evil men are caught in it, but good men stay away and sing for joy.

7 The good man knows the poor man's rights; the godless don't care.

8 Fools start fights everywhere while wise men try to keep peace.

9 There's no use arguing with a fool. He only rages and scoffs, and tempers flare.

10 The godly pray for those who long to kill them.

11 A rebel shouts in anger; a wise man holds his temper in and cools it.

ROMANS 12

6 God has given each of us the ability to do certain things well. So if God has given you the ability to prophesy, then prophesy whenever you can—as often as your faith is strong enough to receive a message from God.

7 If your gift is that of serving others, serve them well. If you are a teacher, do a good job of teaching.

8 If you are a preacher, see to it that your sermons are strong and helpful. If God has given you money, be generous in helping others with it. If God has given you administrative ability and put you in charge of the work of others, take the responsibility seriously. Those who offer comfort to the sorrowing should do so with Christian cheer.

9 Don't just pretend that you love others: really love them. Hate what is wrong. Stand on the side of the good.

10 Love each other with brotherly affection and take delight in honoring each other.

11 Never be lazy in your work but serve the Lord enthusiastically.

12 Be glad for all God is planning for you. Be patient in trouble, and prayerful always.

13 When God's children are in need, you be the one to help them out. And get into the habit of inviting guests home for dinner or, if they need lodging, for the night.

14 If someone mistreats you because you are a Christian, don't curse him; pray that God will bless him.

1 Peter 1

19 . . . He paid for you with the precious lifeblood of Christ, the sinless, spotless Lamb of God.

21 Because of this, your trust can be in God who raised Christ from the dead and gave him great glory. Now your faith and hope can rest in him alone.

22 Now you can have real love for everyone because your souls have been cleansed from selfishness and hatred when you trusted Christ to save you; so see to it that you really do love each other warmly, with all your hearts.

~6~

When You Are Critical, Complaining

Leave judging to God

ROMANS 14

10 You have no right to criticize your brother or look down on him. Remember, each of us will stand personally before the Judgment Seat of God.

11 For it is written, "As I live," says the Lord, "every knee shall bow to me and every tongue confess to God."

12 Yes, each of us will give an account of himself to God.

13 So don't criticize each other any more. Try instead to live in such a way that you will never make your brother stumble by letting him see you doing something he thinks is wrong.

JAMES 3

1 Dear brothers, don't be too eager to tell others their faults, for we all make many mistakes; and when we teachers of religion, who should know better, do wrong, our punishment will be greater than it would be for others.

JAMES 4

11 Don't criticize and speak evil about each other, dear brothers. If you do, you will be fighting against God's law of loving one

another, declaring it is wrong. But your job is not to decide whether this law is right or wrong, but to obey it.

12 Only he who made the law can rightly judge among us. He alone decides to save us or destroy. So what right do you have to judge or criticize others?

JAMES 5

9 Don't grumble about each other, brothers. Are you yourselves above criticism? For see! The great Judge is coming. He is almost here. [Let him do whatever criticizing must be done.]

Caution!

PROVERBS 15

3 The Lord is watching everywhere and keeps his eye on both the evil and the good.

4 Gentle words cause life and health; griping brings discouragement.

PROVERBS 17

1 A dry crust eaten in peace is better than steak every day along with argument and strife.

22 A cheerful heart does good like medicine, but a broken spirit makes one sick.

LUKE 6

35 Love your *enemies!* Do good to *them!* Lend to *them!* And don't be concerned about the fact that they won't repay. Then your reward from heaven will be very great, and you will truly be acting as sons of God: for he is kind to the *unthankful* and to those who are *very wicked.*

36 Try to show as much compassion as your Father does.

37 Never criticize or condemn—or it will all come back on you. Go easy on others; then they will do the same for you.

38 For if you give, you will get! Your gift will return to you in full and overflowing measure, pressed down, shaken together to make room for more, and running over. Whatever measure you use to give—large or small—will be used to measure what is given back to you.

MATTHEW 7

1 Don't criticize, and then you won't be criticized!

2 For others will treat you as you treat them.

3 And why worry about a speck in the eye of a brother when you have a board in your own?

4 Should you say, "Friend, let me help you get that speck out of your eye," when you can't even see because of the board in your own?

5 Hypocrite! First get rid of the board. Then you can see to help your brother.

PHILIPPIANS 2

14 In everything you do, stay away from complaining and arguing.

15 So that no one can speak a word of blame against you. You are to live clean, innocent lives as children of God in a dark world full of people who are crooked and stubborn. Shine out among them like beacon lights.

God gives power to quit complaining

PSALM 39

1 I said to myself, I'm going to quit complaining! I'll keep quiet, especially when the ungodly are around me.

2,3 But as I stood there silently the turmoil within me grew to the bursting point. The more I mused, the hotter the fires inside. Then at last I spoke, and pled with God:

4 Lord, help me to realize how brief my time on earth will be. Help me to know that I am here for but a moment more.

8 Save me from being overpowered by my sins, for even fools will mock me then.

9 Lord, I am speechless before you. I will not open my mouth to speak one word of complaint, for my punishment is from you.

⚌ 7 ⚌

When You Are Envious, Jealous

Some Biblical comments about jealousy and envy

PROVERBS 14

30 A relaxed attitude lengthens a man's life; jealousy rots it away.

PROVERBS 27

4 Jealousy is more dangerous and cruel than anger.

EXODUS 20

17 "You must not be envious of your neighbor's house, or want to sleep with his wife, or want to own his slaves, oxen, donkeys, or anything else he has."

Other thoughts

LUKE 12

31 He will always give you all you need from day to day if you will make the Kingdom of God your primary concern.

JAMES 3

15 For jealousy and selfishness are not God's kind of wisdom. Such things are earthly, unspiritual, inspired by the devil.

16 For wherever there is jealousy or selfish ambition, there will be disorder and every other kind of evil.

17 But the wisdom that comes from heaven is first of all pure and full of quiet gentleness. Then it is peace-loving and courteous. It allows discussion and is willing to yield to others; it is full of mercy and good deeds. It is wholehearted and straightforward and sincere.

PSALM 49

16 So do not be dismayed when evil men grow rich and build their lovely homes.

17 For when they die they carry nothing with them! Their honors will not follow them.

18 Though a man calls himself happy all through his life—and the world loudly applauds success—

19 Yet in the end he dies like everyone else, and enters eternal darkness.

20 For man with all his pomp must die like any animal.

PSALM 37

1 Never envy the wicked!

2 Soon they fade away like grass and disappear.

3 Trust in the Lord instead. Be kind and good to others; then you will live safely here in the land and prosper, feeding in safety.

4 Be delighted with the Lord. Then he will give you all your heart's desires.

7 Rest in the Lord; wait patiently for him to act. Don't be envious of evil men who prosper.

8 Stop your anger! Turn off your wrath. Don't fret and worry—it only leads to harm.

11 But all who humble themselves before the Lord shall be given every blessing, and shall have wonderful peace.

1 PETER 2

1 So get rid of your feelings of hatred. Don't just pretend to be good! Be done with dishonesty and jealousy and talking about others behind their backs.

Don't envy your brother; he may be rich on earth but not in heaven

LUKE 12

13 Then someone called from the crowd, "Sir, please tell my brother to divide my father's estate with me."

14 But Jesus replied, "Man, who made me a judge over you to decide such things as that?

15 Beware! Don't always be wishing for what you don't have. For real life and real living are not related to how rich we are."

16 Then he gave an illustration: "A rich man had a fertile farm that produced fine crops.

17 In fact, his barns were full to overflowing—he couldn't get everything in. He thought about his problem,

18 And finally exclaimed, 'I know—I'll tear down my barns and build bigger ones! Then I'll have room enough.

19 And I'll sit back and say to myself, "Friend, you have enough stored away for years to come. Now take it easy! Wine, women, and song for you!"

20 But God said to him, 'Fool! Tonight you die. Then who will get it all?'

21 "Yes, every man is a fool who gets rich on earth but not in heaven."

∽ 8 ∾

When You Feel Failure, Frustration

God knows all about it and is compassionate

PSALM 139

1 O Lord, you have examined my heart and know everything about me.

2 You know when I sit or stand. When far away you know my every thought.

3 You chart the path ahead of me, and tell me where to stop and rest. Every moment, you know where I am.

4 You know what I am going to say before I even say it.

5 You both precede and follow me, and place your hand of blessing on my head.

6 This is too glorious, too wonderful to believe!

7 I can *never* be lost to your Spirit! I can *never* get away from my God!

8 If I go up to heaven, you are there; if I go down to the place of the dead, you are there.

9 If I ride the morning winds to the farthest oceans,

10 Even there your hand will guide me, your strength will support me.

17,18 How precious it is, Lord, to realize that you are thinking about me constantly! I can't even count how many times a day your thoughts turn towards me. And when I waken in the morning, you are still thinking of me!

DEUTERONOMY 33

26 There is none like the God of Jerusalem—
He descends from the heavens
In majestic splendor to help you.
27 The eternal God is your Refuge,
And underneath are the everlasting arms.

PSALM 103

8 He is merciful and tender toward those who don't deserve it; he is slow to get angry and full of kindness and love.

13 He is like a father to us, tender and sympathetic to those who reverence him.

14 For he knows we are but dust,

15 And that our days are few and brief, like grass, like flowers,

16 Blown by the wind and gone forever.

17,18 But the lovingkindness of the Lord is from everlasting to everlasting, to those who reverence him; his salvation is to children's children of those who are faithful to his covenant and remember to obey him!

1 PETER 5

7 Let him have all your worries and cares, for he is always thinking about you and watching everything that concerns you.

LAMENTATIONS 3

1 I am the man who has seen the afflictions that come from the rod of God's wrath.

2 He has brought me into deepest darkness, shutting out all light.

9 He has shut me into a place of high, smooth walls; he has filled my path with detours.

15 He has filled me with bitterness, and given me a cup of deepest sorrows to drink.

17 O Lord, all peace and all prosperity have long since gone, for you have taken them away. I have forgotten what enjoyment is.

18 All hope is gone; my strength has turned to water, for the Lord has left me.

21 *Yet there is one ray of hope:*

22 *his compassion never ends.* It is only the Lord's mercies that have kept us from complete destruction.

23 Great is his faithfulness; his lovingkindness begins afresh each day.

24 My soul claims the Lord as my inheritance; therefore I will hope in him.

25 The Lord is wonderfully good to those who wait for him, to those who seek for him.

26 It is good both to hope and wait quietly for the salvation of the Lord.

Prayers for help in time of failure and frustration

PSALM 40

1 I waited patiently for God to help me; then he listened and heard my cry.

2 He lifted me out of the pit of despair, out from the bog and the mire, and set my feet on a hard, firm path and steadied me as I walked along.

3 He has given me a new song to sing, of praises to our God. Now many will hear of the glorious things he did for me, and stand in awe before the Lord, and put their trust in him.

4 Many blessings are given to those who trust the Lord, and have no confidence in those who are proud, or who trust in idols.

5 O Lord my God, many and many a time you have done great miracles for us, and we are ever in your thoughts. Who else can do such glorious things? No one else can be compared with you. There isn't time to tell of all your wonderful deeds.

11 O Lord, don't hold back your tender mercies from me! My only hope is in your love and faithfulness.

12 Otherwise I perish, for problems far too big for me to solve are piled higher than my head. Meanwhile my sins, too many to count, have all caught up with me and I am ashamed to look up. My heart quails within me.

13 Please, Lord, rescue me! Quick! Come and help me!

17 I am poor and needy, yet the Lord is thinking about me right now! O my God, you are my helper. You are my Savior; come quickly, and save me. Please don't delay!

PSALM 31

1 Lord, I trust in you alone. Don't let my enemies defeat me. Rescue me because you are the God who always does what is right.

2 Answer quickly when I cry to you; bend low and hear my whispered plea. Be for me a great Rock of safety from my foes.

3 Yes, you are my Rock and my fortress; honor your name by leading me out of this peril.

5,6 Into your hand I commit my spirit.

PSALM 61

1 O God, listen to me! Hear my prayer!

2 For wherever I am, though far away at the ends of the earth, I will cry to you for help. When my heart is faint and overwhelmed, lead me to the mighty, towering Rock of safety.

3 For You are my refuge, a high tower where my enemies can never reach me.

8 And I will praise your name continually, fulfilling my vow of praising you each day.

PSALM 62

1 I stand silently before the Lord, waiting for him to rescue me. For salvation comes from him alone.

2 Yes, he alone is my Rock, my rescuer, defense and fortress. Why then should I be tense with fear when troubles come?

7 My protection and success come from God alone. He is my refuge, a Rock where no enemy can reach me.

8 O my people, trust him all the time. Pour out your longings before him, for he can help!

9 The greatest of men, or the lowest—both alike are nothing in his sight. They weigh less than air on scales.

For comfort in time of failure and frustration

2 TIMOTHY 2

13 Even when we are too weak to have any faith left, He remains faithful to us, for He cannot disown us as we are part of Himself, and He will always carry out His promises to us.

PSALM 37

23 The steps of good men are directed by the Lord. He delights in each step they take.

24 If they fall it isn't fatal, for the Lord holds them with his hand.

1 PETER 4

12 Dear friends, don't be bewildered or surprised when you go through the fiery trials ahead, for this is no strange, unusual thing that is going to happen to you.

13 Instead, be really glad—because these trials will make you partners with Christ in his suffering, and afterwards you will have the wonderful joy of sharing his glory in that coming day when it will be displayed.

19 So if you are suffering according to God's will, keep on doing what is right and trust yourself to the God who made you, for he will never fail you.

HEBREWS 13

5b ... For God has said, "I will never, *never* fail you nor forsake you."

6 That is why we can say without any doubt or fear, "The Lord is my Helper and I am not afraid of anything that mere man can do to me."

2 CHRONICLES 16

9 For the eyes of the Lord search back and forth across the whole earth, looking for people whose hearts are perfect toward him, so that he can show his great power in helping them.

EPHESIANS 1

19 I pray that you will begin to understand how incredibly great his power is to help those who believe him. It is that same mighty power

20 That raised Christ from the dead and seated him in the place of honor at God's right hand in heaven.

PSALM 27

1 The Lord is my light and my salvation; whom shall I fear?

2 When evil men come to destroy me, they will stumble and fall!

3 Yes, though a mighty army marches against me, my heart shall know no fear! I am confident that God will save me.

4 The one thing I want from God, the thing I seek most of all, is the privilege of meditating in his Temple, living in his presence every day of my life, delighting in his incomparable perfections and glory.

7 Listen to my pleading, Lord! Be merciful and send the help I need.

8 My heart has heard you say, "Come and talk with me, O my people." And my heart responds, "Lord, I am coming."

9 Oh, do not hide yourself when I am trying to find you. Do not angrily reject your servant. You have been my help in all my trials before; don't leave me now. Don't forsake me, O God of my salvation.

10 For if my father and mother should abandon me, you would welcome and comfort me.

13 I am expecting the Lord to rescue me again, so that once again I will see his goodness to me here in the land of the living.

14 Don't be impatient. Wait for the Lord, and he will come and save you! Be brave, stouthearted and courageous. Yes, wait and he will help you.

PSALM 91

1 We live within the shadow of the Almighty, sheltered by the God who is above all gods.

2 This I declare, that he alone is my refuge, my place of safety; he is my God, and I am trusting him.

3 For he rescues you from every trap, and protects you from the fatal plague.

4 He will shield you with his wings! They will shelter you. His faithful promises are your armor.

5 Now you don't need to be afraid of the dark any more, nor fear the dangers of the day;

6 Nor dread the plagues of darkness, nor disasters in the morning.

7 Though a thousand fall at my side, though ten thousand are dying around me, the evil will not touch me.

8 I will see how the wicked are punished but I will not share it.

9 For Jehovah is my refuge! I choose the God above all gods to shelter me.

10 How then can evil overtake me or any plague come near?

11 For he orders his angels to protect you wherever you go.

12 They will steady you with their hands to keep you from stumbling against the rocks on the trail.

13 You can safely meet a lion or step on poisonous snakes, yes, even trample them beneath your feet!

14 For the Lord says, "Because he loves me, I will rescue him; I will make him great because he trusts in my name.

15 When he calls on me I will answer; I will be with him in trouble, and rescue him and honor him.

16 I will satisfy him with a full life and give him my salvation."

There may be a purpose in your failure or frustration

ISAIAH 30

18 Yet the Lord still waits for you to come to him, so he can show you his love; he will conquer you to bless you, just as he said. For the Lord is faithful to his promises. Blessed are all those who wait for him to help them.

1 PETER 1

6 So be truly glad! There is wonderful joy ahead, even though the going is rough for a while down here.

7 These trials are only to test your faith, to see whether or not it is strong and pure. It is being tested as fire tests gold and purifies it—and your faith is far more precious to God than mere gold; so if your faith remains strong after being tried in the test tube of fiery trials, it will bring you much praise and glory and honor on the day of his return.

Help and guidance for a better future

PROVERBS 3

1,2 My son, never forget the things I've taught you. If you want a long and satisfying life, closely follow my instructions.

3 Never forget to be truthful and kind. Hold these virtues tightly. Write them deep within your heart.

4,5 If you want favor with both God and man, and a reputation for good judgment and common sense, then trust the Lord completely; don't ever trust yourself.

6 In everything you do, put God first, and he will direct you and crown your efforts with success.

1 THESSALONIANS 5

16 Always be joyful.

17 Always keep on praying.

18 No matter what happens, always be thankful, for this is God's will for you who belong to Christ Jesus.

COLOSSIANS 2

6 And now just as you trusted Christ to save you, trust him, too, for each day's problems; live in vital union with him.

7 Let your roots grow down into him and draw up nourishment from him. See that you go on growing in the Lord, and become strong and vigorous in the truth you were taught. Let your lives overflow with joy and thanksgiving for all he has done.

8 Don't let others spoil your faith and joy with their philosophies, their wrong and shallow answers built on men's thoughts and ideas, instead of on what Christ has said.

9 For in Christ there is all of God in a human body;

10 *So you have everything when you have Christ*, and you are filled with God through your union with Christ. He is the highest Ruler, with authority over every other power.

MATTHEW 6

34 So don't be anxious about tomorrow. God will take care of your tomorrow too. Live one day at a time.

PSALM 31

19 Oh, how great is your goodness to those who publicly declare that you will rescue them. For you have stored up great blessings for those who trust and reverence you.

PHILIPPIANS 4

8 And now, brothers, as I close this letter let me say this one more thing: Fix your thoughts on what is true and good and right. Think about things that are pure and lovely, and dwell on the fine, good things in others. Think about all you can praise God for and be glad about.

9 Keep putting into practice all you learned from me and saw me doing, and the God of peace will be with you.

12 I know how to live on almost nothing or with everything. I have learned the secret of contentment in every situation, whether it be a full stomach or hunger, plenty or want;

13 For I can do everything God asks me to with the help of Christ who gives me the strength and power.

~9~

When You Feel God Is Far Away

Every moment God knows where you are

PSALM 139

1 O Lord, you have examined my heart and know everything about me.

2 You know when I sit or stand. When far away you know my every thought.

3 You chart the path ahead of me, and tell me where to stop and rest. Every moment, you know where I am.

4 You know what I am going to say before I even say it.

5 You both precede and follow me, and place your hand of blessing on my head.

6 This is too glorious, too wonderful to believe!

7 I can *never* be lost to your Spirit! I can *never* get away from my God!

8 If I go up to heaven, you are there; if I go down to the place of the dead, you are there.

9 If I ride the morning winds to the farthest oceans,

10 Even there your hand will guide me, your strength will support me.

11 If I try to hide in the darkness, the night becomes light around me.

12 For even darkness cannot hide from God; to you the night shines as bright as day. Darkness and light are both alike to you.

13 You made all the delicate, inner parts of my body, and knit them together in my mother's womb.

14 Thank you for making me so wonderfully complex! It is amazing to think about. Your workmanship is marvelous—and how well I know it.

15 You were there while I was being formed in utter seclusion!

16 You saw me before I was born and scheduled each day of my life before I began to breathe. Every day was recorded in your Book!

17,18 How precious it is, Lord, to realize that you are thinking about me constantly! I can't even count how many times a day your thoughts turn towards me. And when I waken in the morning, you are still thinking of me!

PSALM 121

3,4 He will never let me stumble, slip or fall. For he is always watching, never sleeping.

5 Jehovah himself is caring for you! He is your defender.

6 He protects you day and night.

7 He keeps you from all evil, and preserves your life.

8 He keeps his eye upon you as you come and go, and always guards you.

How close can God get? He has stationed the Holy Spirit inside believers

2 CORINTHIANS 1

22 He has put his brand upon us—his mark of ownership—and given us his Holy Spirit in our hearts as guarantee that we belong to him, and as the first installment of all that he is going to give us.

JAMES 4

4 Don't you realize that making friends with God's enemies—the evil pleasures of this world—makes you an enemy of God? I say it again, that if your aim is to enjoy the evil pleasure of the unsaved world, you cannot also be a friend of God.

5 Or what do you think the Scripture means when it says that the Holy Spirit, whom God has placed within us, watches over us with tender jealousy?

6 But he gives us more and more strength to stand against all such evil longings. As the Scripture says, God gives strength to the humble, but sets himself against the proud and haughty.

7 So give yourselves humbly to God. Resist the devil and he will flee from you.

8 And when you draw close to God, God will draw close to you. Wash your hands, you sinners, and let your hearts be filled with God alone to make them pure and true to him.

God, You are holding my right hand

PSALM 73

23 But even so, you love me! You are holding my right hand!

24 You will keep on guiding me all my life with your wisdom and counsel; and afterwards receive me into the glories of heaven!

25 Whom have I in heaven but you? And I desire no one on earth as much as you!

26 My health fails; my spirits droop, yet God remains! He is the strength of my heart; he is mine forever!

HEBREWS 13

5b . . . For God has said, "I will never, *never* fail you nor forsake you."

6 That is why we can say without any doubt or fear, "The Lord is my Helper and I am not afraid of anything man can do to me."

He knows the number of hairs on your head

LUKE 12

6 What is the price of five sparrows? A couple of pennies? Not much more than that. Yet God does not forget a single one of them.

7 And he knows the number of hairs on your head! Never fear, you are far more valuable to him than a whole flock of sparrows.

Promises

REVELATION 3

20 Look! I have been standing at the door and I am constantly knocking. If anyone hears me calling him and opens the door, I will come in and fellowship with him and he with me.

HEBREWS 7

19b . . . For Christ makes us acceptable to God, and now we may draw near to him.

HEBREWS 2

11 We who have been made holy by Jesus, now have the same Father he has. That is why Jesus is not ashamed to call us his brothers.

12 For he says in the book of Psalms, "I will talk to my brothers about God my Father, and together we will sing his praises."

ACTS 2

25b . . . I know the Lord is always with me. He is helping me. God's mighty power supports me.

Lack of faith

2 TIMOTHY 2

13 Even when we are too weak to have any faith left, he remains faithful to us and will help us, for he cannot disown us who are part of himself, and he will always carry out his promises to us.

JOHN 15

16 You didn't choose me! I chose you! I appointed you to go and produce lovely fruit always, so that no matter what you ask for from the Father, using my name, he will give it to you.

In Him we live and move and have our being

PSALM 66

8 Let everyone bless God and sing his praises,

9 For he holds our lives in his hands! And he holds our feet to the path!

16 Come and hear, all of you who reverence the Lord, and I will tell you what he did for me:

17 For I cried to him for help, with praises ready on my tongue.

18 He would not have listened if I had not confessed my sins.

19 But he listened! He heard my prayer! He paid attention to it!

20 Blessed be God who didn't turn away when I was praying, and didn't refuse me his kindness and love.

ACTS 17

24 He made the world and everything in it, and since he is Lord of heaven and earth, he doesn't live in man-made temples;

25 And human hands can't minister to his needs—for he has no needs! He himself gives life and breath to everything, and satisfies every need there is.

26 He created all the people of the world from one man, Adam, and scattered the nations across the face of the earth. He decided beforehand which should rise and fall, and when. He determined their boundaries.

27 His purpose in all of this is that they should seek after God, and perhaps feel their way toward him and find him—though he is not far from any one of us.

28 For in him we live and move and are! As one of your own poets says it, 'We are the sons of God.'

God cleared a path for you to come to Him

Colossians 1

20 It was through what his Son did that God cleared a path for everything to come to him—all things in heaven and on earth—for Christ's death on the cross has made peace with God for all by his blood.

21 This includes you who were once so far away from God. You were his enemies and hated him and were separated from him by your evil thoughts and actions, yet now he has brought you back as his friends.

22 He has done this through the death on the cross of his own human body, and now as a result Christ has brought you into the very presence of God, and you are standing there before him with nothing left against you—nothing left that he could even chide you for;

23 The only condition is that you fully believe the Truth, standing in it steadfast and firm, strong in the Lord, convinced of the Good News that Jesus died for you, and never shifting from trusting him to save you.

❧10❧

When You Feel Guilty And Sinful

God can forgive your sins

HEBREWS 6

16 When a man takes an oath, he is calling upon someone greater than himself to force him to do what he has promised, or to punish him if he later refuses to do it; the oath ends all argument about it.

17 God also bound himself with an oath, so that those he promised to help would be perfectly sure and never need to wonder whether he might change his plans.

18 He has given us both his promise and his oath, two things we can completely count on, for it is impossible for God to tell a lie. Now all those who flee to him to save them can take new courage when they hear such assurances from God; now they can know without doubt that he will give them the salvation he has promised them.

19 This certain hope of being saved is a strong and trustworthy anchor for our souls, connecting us with God himself behind the sacred curtains of heaven,

20 where Christ has gone ahead to plead for us from his position as our High Priest, with the honor and rank of Melchizedek.

JOHN 5

24 "I say emphatically that anyone who listens to my message and believes in God who sent me has eternal life, and will never be damned for his sins, but has already passed out of death into life."

JOHN 3

16 For God loved the world so much that he gave his only Son so that anyone who believes in him shall not perish but have eternal life.

17 God did not send his Son into the world to condemn it, but to save it.

18 There is no eternal doom awaiting those who trust him to save them.

COLOSSIANS 1

20 It was through what his Son did that God cleared a path for everything to come to him—all things in heaven and on earth—for Christ's death on the cross has made peace with God for all by his blood.

21 This includes you who were once so far away from God. You were his enemies and hated him and were separated from him by your evil thoughts and actions, yet now he has brought you back as his friends.

22 He has done this through the death on the cross of his own human body, and now as a result Christ has brought you into the very presence of God, and you are standing there before him with nothing left against you—nothing left that he could even chide you for;

23 The only condition is that you fully believe the Truth, standing in it steadfast and firm, strong in the Lord, convinced of the Good News that Jesus died for you, and never shifting from trusting him to save you.

EPHESIANS 1

4 Long ago, even before he made the world, God chose us to be his very own, through what Christ would do for us; he decided then to make us holy in his eyes, without a single fault—we who stand before him covered with his love.

5 His unchanging plan has always been to adopt us into his own family by sending Jesus Christ to die for us. And he did this because he wanted to!

PSALM 103

1 I bless the holy name of God with all my heart.

2 Yes, I will bless the Lord and not forget the glorious things he does for me.

3 He forgives all my sins. He heals me.

8 He is merciful and tender toward those who don't deserve it; he is slow to get angry and full of kindness and love.

9 He never bears a grudge, nor remains angry forever.

10 He has not punished us as we deserve for all our sins,

11 For his mercy toward those who fear and honor him is as great as the height of the heavens above the earth.

12 He has removed our sins as far away from us as the east is from the west.

ECCLESIASTES 7

20 And there is not a single man in all the earth who is always good and never sins.

1 CORINTHIANS 1

8 And he guarantees right up to the end that you will be counted free from all sin and guilt on that day when he returns.

9 God will surely do this for you, for he always does just what he says, and he is the one who invited you into this wonderful friendship with his Son, even Christ our Lord.

JUDE 1

24,25 And now—all glory to him who alone is God, who saves us through Jesus Christ our Lord; yes, splendor and majesty, all power and authority are his from the beginning; his they are and his they evermore shall be. And he is able to keep you from slipping and falling away, and to bring you, sinless and perfect, into his glorious presence with mighty shouts of everlasting joy. Amen.

When you can't forgive yourself

COLOSSIANS 2

11 When you came to Christ he set you free from your evil desires, not by a bodily operation of circumcision but by a spiritual operation, the baptism of your souls.

12 For in baptism you see how your old, evil nature died with him and was buried with him; and then you came up out of death with him into a new life because you trusted the Word of the mighty God who raised Christ from the dead.

13 You were dead in sins, and your sinful desires were not yet cut away. Then he gave you a share in the very life of Christ, for he forgave all your sins,

14 And blotted out the charges proved against you, the list of his commandments which you had not obeyed. He took this list of sins and destroyed it by nailing it to Christ's cross.

15 In this way God took away Satan's power to accuse you of sin, and God openly displayed to the whole world Christ's triumph at the cross where your sins were all taken away.

2 CORINTHIANS 5

17 When someone becomes a Christian he becomes a brand new person inside. He is not the same any more. A new life has begun!

18 All these new things are from God who brought us back to himself through what Christ Jesus did. And God has given us the privilege of urging everyone to come into his favor and be reconciled to him.

19 For God was in Christ, restoring the world to himself, no longer counting men's sins against them but blotting them out. This is the wonderful message he has given us to tell others.

21 For God took the sinless Christ and poured into him our sins. Then, in exchange, he poured God's goodness into us!

ROMANS 8

29 For from the very beginning God decided that those who came to him—and all along he knew who would—should become like his Son, so that his Son would be the First, with many brothers.

30 And having chosen us, he called us to come to him; and when we came, he declared us "not guilty," filled us with Christ's goodness, gave us right standing with himself, and promised us his glory.

33 Who dares accuse us whom God has chosen for his own? Will God? No! He is the one who has forgiven us and given us right standing with himself.

34 Who then will condemn us? Will Christ? *No!* For he is the one who died for us and came back to life again for us and is sitting at the place of highest honor next to God, pleading for us there in heaven.

The "how" of being forgiven

ROMANS 3

20 Now do you see it? No one can ever be made right in God's sight by doing what the law commands. For the more we know of God's laws, the clearer it becomes that we aren't obeying them; his laws serve only to make us see that we are sinners.

21,22 But now God has shown us a different way to heaven—not by "being good enough" and trying to keep his laws, but by a new way (though not new, really, for the Scriptures told about it long ago). Now God says he will accept and acquit us—declare us "not guilty"—if we trust Jesus Christ to take away our sins. And we all can be saved in this same way, by coming to Christ, no matter who we are or what we have been like.

23 Yes, all have sinned; all fall short of God's glorious ideal;

24 Yet now God declares us "not guilty" of offending him if we trust in Jesus Christ, who in his kindness freely takes away our sins.

25 For God sent Christ Jesus to take the punishment for our sins and to end all God's anger against us. He used Christ's blood and our faith as the means of saving us from his wrath.

26 And now in these days also He can receive sinners in this same way, because Jesus took away their sins.

27 Then what can we boast about doing, to earn our salvation? Nothing at all. Why? Because our acquittal is not based on our good deeds; it is based on what Christ has done and our faith in him.

28 So it is that we are saved by faith in Christ and not by the good things we do.

31 Well then, if we are saved by faith, does this mean that we no longer need obey God's laws? Just the opposite! In fact, only when we trust Jesus can we truly obey him.

Acts 13

38 Brothers! Listen! In this man Jesus, there is forgiveness for your sins!

39 Everyone who trusts in him is freed from all guilt and declared righteous.

1 John 1

8 If we say that we have no sin, we are only fooling ourselves, and refusing to accept the truth.

9 But if we confess our sins to him, he can be depended on to forgive us and to cleanse us from every wrong. [And it is perfectly proper for God to do this for us because Christ died to wash away our sins.]

67

Examples of God's forgiveness

PSALM 32

1 What happiness for those whose guilt has been forgiven! What joys when sins are covered over! What relief for those who have confessed their sins and God has cleared their record.

3 There was a time when I wouldn't admit what a sinner I was. But my dishonesty made me miserable and filled my days with frustration.

4 All day and all night your hand was heavy on me. My strength evaporated like water on a sunny day

5 Until I finally admitted all my sins to you and stopped trying to hide them. I said to myself, "I will confess them to the Lord." And you forgave me! All my guilt is gone.

6 Now I say that each believer should confess his sins to God when he is aware of them, while there is time to be forgiven. Judgment will not touch him if he does.

LUKE 23

32,33 Two others, criminals, were led out to be executed with him at a place called "The Skull." There all three were crucified—Jesus on the center cross, and the two criminals on either side.

34 "Father, forgive these people," Jesus said, "for they don't know what they are doing."

JOHN 8

1 Jesus returned to the Mount of Olives.

2 But early the next morning he was back again at the Temple. A crowd soon gathered, and he sat down and talked to them.

3 As he was speaking, the Jewish leaders and Pharisees brought a woman caught in adultery and placed her out in front of the staring crowd.

4 "Teacher," they said to Jesus, "this woman was caught in the very act of adultery.

5 Moses' law says to kill her. What about it?"

7 They kept demanding an answer, so he stood up again and said, "All right, hurl the stones at her until she dies. But only he who never sinned may throw the first!"

9 And the Jewish leaders slipped away one by one, beginning with the eldest, until only Jesus was left in front of the crowd with the woman.

10 Then Jesus stood up again and said to her, "Where are your accusers? Didn't even one of them condemn you?"

11 "No, sir," she said.
And Jesus said, "Neither do I. Go and sin no more."

LUKE 15

11 A man had two sons.

12 When the younger told his father, "I want my share of your estate now, instead of waiting until you die!" his father agreed to divide his wealth between his sons.

13 A few days later this younger son packed all his belongings and took a trip to a distant land, and there wasted all his money on parties and prostitutes.

14 About the time his money was gone a great famine swept over the land, and he began to starve.

15 He persuaded a local farmer to hire him to feed his pigs.

16 The boy became so hungry that even the pods he was feeding the swine looked good to him. And no one gave him anything.

17,18 When he finally came to his senses, he said to himself, "At home even the hired men have food enough and to spare, and here I am, dying of hunger! I will go home to my father and say, 'Father, I have sinned against both heaven and you,

19 I am no longer worthy of being called your son. Please take me on as a hired man.' "

20 So he returned home to his father. And while he was still a long distance away, his father saw him coming, and was filled with loving pity and ran and embraced him and kissed him.

21 His son said to him, "Father, I have sinned against heaven and you, and am not worthy of being called your son—"

22 But his father said to the slaves, "Quick! Bring the finest robe in the house and put it on him. And a jeweled ring for his finger; and shoes!

23 And kill the calf we have in the fattening pen. We must celebrate with a feast,

24 For this son of mine was dead and has returned to life . . ."

How to pray for forgiveness

PSALM 130

1 O Lord, from the depths of despair I cry for your help:

2 "Hear me! Answer! Help me!"

3,4 Lord, if you keep in mind our sins then who can ever get an answer to his prayers? But you forgive! What an awesome thing this is!

5 That is why I wait expectantly, trusting God to help, for he has promised.

PSALM 86

5 O Lord, you are so good and kind, so ready to forgive; so full of mercy for all who ask your aid.

PSALM 51

1 O loving and kind God, have mercy. Have pity upon me and take away the awful stain of my transgressions.

2 Oh, wash me, cleanse me from this guilt. Let me be pure again.

3 For I admit my shameful deed—it haunts me day and night.

4 It is against you and you alone I sinned, and did this terrible thing. You saw it all, and your sentence against me is just.

7 Sprinkle me with the cleansing blood and I shall be clean again. Wash me and I shall be whiter than snow.

∼ 11 ∼

When You Feel Happy

Who is happy?

PSALM 144

15 Yes, happy are those whose God is Jehovah.

MATTHEW 5

1,2 One day as the crowds were gathering, he went up the hill-side with his disciples and sat down and taught them there.

3 "Humble men are very fortunate!" he told them, "for the Kingdom of Heaven is given to them.

4 Those who mourn are fortunate! for they shall be comforted.

5 The meek and lowly are fortunate! for the whole wide world belongs to them.

6 Happy are those who long to be just and good, for they shall be completely satisfied.

7 Happy are the kind and merciful, for they shall be shown mercy.

8 Happy are those whose hearts are pure, for they shall see God.

9 Happy are those who strive for peace—they shall be called the sons of God.

10 Happy are those who are persecuted because they are good, for the Kingdom of Heaven is theirs.

11 When you are reviled and persecuted and lied about because you are my followers—wonderful!

12 Be *happy* about it! Be *very glad!* for a *tremendous reward* awaits you up in heaven. And remember, the ancient prophets were persecuted too.

PSALM 33

20 We depend upon the Lord alone to save us. Only he can help us; he protects us like a shield.

21 No wonder we are happy in the Lord! For we are trusting him. We trust his holy name.

PSALM 106

3 Happiness comes to those who are fair to others and are always just and good.

PSALM 104

33 I will sing to the Lord as long as I live. I will praise God to my last breath!

34 May he be pleased by all these thoughts about him, for he is the source of all my joy.

35 Let all sinners perish—all who refuse to praise him. But I will praise him. Hallelujah!

JOHN 15

9 I have loved you even as the Father has loved me. Live within my love.

10 When you obey me you are living in my love, just as I obey my Father and live in his love.

11 I have told you this so that you will be filled with my joy. Yes, your cup of joy will overflow!

12 I demand that you love each other as much as I love you.

PSALM 32

1,2 What happiness for those whose guilt has been forgiven! What joys when sins are covered over! What relief for those who have confessed their sins and God has cleared their record.

PSALM 119

1 Happy are all who perfectly follow the laws of God.
2 Happy are all who search for God, and always do his will.

Sing praises of joy!

JAMES 5

13b . . . And those who have reason to be thankful should continually be singing praises to the Lord.

PSALM 148

1 Praise the Lord, O heavens! Praise him from the skies!
2 Praise him, all his angels, all the armies of heaven.
3 Praise him sun and moon, and all you twinkling stars.
4 Praise him, skies above. Praise him, vapors high above the clouds.
5 Let everything he has made give praise to him! For he issued his command, and they came into being;
6 He established them forever and forever. His orders will never be revoked.
7 And praise him down here on earth, you creatures of the ocean depths.
8 Let fire and hail, snow, rain, wind and weather, all obey.
9 Let the mountains and hills, the fruit trees and cedars,
10 The wild animals and cattle, the snakes and birds,
11 The kings and all the people, with their rulers and their judges,

THE LIVING BIBLE SPEAKS TO YOU

12 Young men and maidens, old men and children—

13 All praise the Lord together. For he alone is worthy. His glory is far greater than all of earth and heaven.

PSALM 8

1 O Lord our God, the majesty and glory of your name fills all the earth and overflows the heavens.

2 You have taught the little children to praise you perfectly. May their example shame and silence your enemies!

3 When I look up into the night skies and see the work of your fingers—the moon and the stars you have made—

4 I cannot understand how you can bother with mere puny man, to pay any attention to him!

5 And yet you have made him only a little lower than the angels, and placed a crown of glory and honor upon his head.

6 You have put him in charge of everything you made; everything is put under his authority:

7 All sheep and oxen, and wild animals too,

8 The birds and fish, and all the life in the sea.

9 O Jehovah, our Lord, the majesty and glory of your name fills the earth.

PSALM 96

1 Sing a new song to the Lord! Sing it everywhere around the world!

2 Sing out his praises! Bless his name. Each day tell someone that he saves.

3 Publish his glorious acts throughout the earth. Tell everyone about the amazing things he does.

4 For the Lord is great beyond description, and greatly to be praised. Worship only him among the gods!

11 Let the heavens be glad, the earth rejoice; let the vastness of the roaring seas demonstrate his glory.

12 Praise him for the growing fields, for they display his greatness. Let the trees of the forest rustle with praise.

PSALM 108

1 O God, my heart is ready to praise you! I will sing and rejoice before you.

2 Wake up, O harp and lyre! We will meet the dawn with song.

3 I will praise you everywhere around the world, in every nation.

4 For your lovingkindness is great beyond measure, high as the heavens. Your faithfulness reaches the skies.

5 His glory is far more vast than the heavens. It towers above the earth.

PSALM 98

1 Sing a new song to the Lord telling about his mighty deeds! For he has won a mighty victory by his power and holiness.

5 Sing your praise accompanied by music from the harp.

6 Let the cornets and trumpets shout! Make a joyful symphony before the Lord, the King!

7 Let the sea in all its vastness roar with praise! Let the earth and all those living on it shout, "Glory to the Lord."

8,9 Let the waves clap their hands in glee, and the hills sing out their songs of joy before the Lord, for he is coming to judge the world with perfect justice.

PSALM 100

1 Shout with joy before the Lord, O earth!

2 Obey him gladly; come before him, singing with joy.

3 Try to realize what this means—the Lord is God! He made us—we are his people, the sheep of his pasture.

4 Go through his open gates with great thanksgiving; enter his courts with praise. Give thanks to him and bless his name.

5 For the Lord is always good. He is always loving and kind, and his faithfulness goes on and on to each succeeding generation.

PSALM 150

1 Hallelujah! Yes, praise the Lord! Praise him in his Temple, and in the heavens he made with mighty power.

2 Praise him for his mighty works. Praise his unequaled greatness.

3 Praise him with the trumpet and with lute and harp.

4 Praise him with the tambourines and processional. Praise him with stringed instruments and horns.

5 Praise him with the cymbals, yes, loud clanging cymbals.

6 Let everything alive give praises to the Lord! *You* praise him! Hallelujah!

PSALM 95

1 Oh, come, let us sing to the Lord! Give a joyous shout in honor of the Rock of our salvation!

2 Come before him with thankful hearts. Let us sing him psalms of praise.

3 For the Lord is a great God, the great King of all gods.

4 He controls the formation of the depths of the earth and the mightiest mountains; all are his.

5 He made the sea and formed the land; they too are his.

6 Come, kneel before the Lord our Maker,

7 For he is our God. We are his sheep and he is our Shepherd. Oh, that you would hear him calling you today and come to him!

∼12∼

When You Feel Hate,
Bear A Grudge

Hate destroys friendships

PROVERBS 18

19 It is harder to win back the friendship of an offended brother than to capture a fortified city . . .

Hate destroys spirituality

HEBREWS 12

15b . . . Watch out that no bitterness takes root among you, for as it springs up it causes deep trouble, hurting many in their spiritual lives.

Christ never even hated His executioners; He is your example

1 PETER 2

22 He never sinned, never told a lie,
23 Never answered back when insulted; when he suffered he did not threaten to get even; he left his case in the hands of God who always judges fairly.

EPHESIANS 5

1 Follow God's example in everything you do just as a much loved child imitates his father.

2 Be full of love for others, following the example of Christ who loved you and gave himself to God as a sacrifice to take away your sins. And God was pleased, for Christ's love for you was like sweet perfume to him.

LUKE 23

32,33 Two others, criminals, were led out to be executed with him at a place called "The Skull." There all three were crucified— Jesus on the center cross, and the two criminals on either side.

34 "Father, forgive these people," Jesus said, "for they don't know what they are doing."

What Jesus said

MATTHEW 18

21 Then Peter came to him and asked, "Sir, how often should I forgive a brother who sins against me? Seven times?"

22 "No!" Jesus replied, "seventy times seven!"

LUKE 17

3b ... "Rebuke your brother if he sins, and forgive him if he is sorry.

4 Even if he wrongs you seven times a day and each time turns again and asks forgiveness, forgive him."

MATTHEW 6

9 Pray along these lines: 'Our Father in heaven, we honor your holy name.

10 We ask that your kingdom will come now. May your will be done here on earth, just as it is in heaven.

11 Give us our food again today, as usual,

12 and forgive us our sins, just as we have forgiven those who have sinned against us.

13 Don't bring us into temptation, but deliver us from the Evil One. Amen.'

14,15 Your heavenly Father will forgive you if you forgive those who sin against you; but if *you* refuse to forgive *them*, *he* will not forgive *you*.

What Paul said

EPHESIANS 4

22 Then throw off your old evil nature—the old you that was a partner in your evil ways—rotten through and through, full of lust and sham.

23 Now your attitudes and thoughts must all be constantly changing for the better.

24 Yes, you must be a new and different person, holy and good. Clothe yourself with this new nature.

26 If you are angry, don't sin by nursing your grudge. Don't let the sun go down with you still angry—get over it quickly;

27 For when you are angry you give a mighty foothold to the devil.

28 If anyone is stealing he must stop it and begin using those hands of his for honest work so he can give to others in need.

31 Stop being mean, bad-tempered and angry. Quarreling, harsh words, and dislike of others should have no place in your lives.

32 Instead, be kind to each other, tenderhearted, forgiving one another, just as God has forgiven you because you belong to Christ.

ROMANS 12

14 If someone mistreats you because you are a Christian, don't curse him; pray that God will bless him.

17 Never pay back evil for evil. Do things in such a way that everyone can see you are honest clear through.

18 Don't quarrel with anyone. Be at peace with everyone, just as much as possible.

19 Dear friends, never avenge yourselves. Leave that to God, for he has said that he will repay those who deserve it.

20 Instead, feed your enemy if he is hungry. If he is thirsty give him something to drink and you will be "heaping coals of fire on his head." In other words, he will feel ashamed of himself for what he has done to you.

21 Don't let evil get the upper hand but conquer evil by doing good.

Some powerful thoughts

COLOSSIANS 3

13 Be gentle and ready to forgive; never hold grudges. Remember, the Lord forgave you, so you must forgive others.

1 JOHN 4

20 If anyone says "I love God," but keeps on hating his brother, he is a liar; for if he doesn't love his brother who is right there in front of him, how can he love God whom he has never seen?

21 And God himself has said that one must love not only God, but his brother too.

HEBREWS 10

30 For we know him who said, "Justice belongs to me; I will repay them"; who also said, "The Lord himself will handle these cases."

31 It is a fearful thing to fall into the hands of the living God.

PROVERBS 25

21,22 If your enemy is hungry, give him food! If he is thirsty, give him something to drink! This will make him feel ashamed of himself, and God will reward you.

2 CORINTHIANS 2

11 A further reason for forgiveness is to keep from being out-smarted by Satan.

ᴄ≈13≈ᴄ

When You Feel Hurt, Humiliated

PSALM 34

18 The Lord is close to those whose hearts are breaking; he rescues those who are humbly sorry for their sins.

19 The good man does not escape all troubles—he has them too. But the Lord helps him in each and every one.

PSALM 33

18,19 But the eyes of the Lord are watching over those who fear him, who rely upon his steady love. He will keep them from death even in times of famine!

20 We depend upon the Lord alone to save us. Only he can help us; he protects us like a shield.

21 No wonder we are happy in the Lord! For we are trusting him. We trust his holy name.

22 Yes, Lord, let your constant love surround us, for our hopes are in you alone.

PSALM 18

2 The Lord is my fort where I can enter and be safe; no one can follow me in and slay me. He is a rugged mountain where I hide; he is my Savior, a rock where none can reach me, and a tower of safety. He is my shield. He is like the strong horn of a mighty fighting bull.

1 PETER 2

19 Praise the Lord if you are punished for doing right!

20 Of course, you get no credit for being patient if you are beaten for doing wrong; but if you do right and suffer for it, and are patient beneath the blows, God is well pleased.

21 This suffering is all part of the work God has given you. Christ, who suffered for you, is your example. Follow in his steps:

22 He never sinned, never told a lie,

23 Never answered back when insulted; when he suffered he did not threaten to get even; he left his case in the hands of God who always judges fairly.

24 He personally carried the load of our sins in his own body when he died on the cross, so that we can be finished with sin and live a good life from now on. For his wounds have healed ours!

1 PETER 3

13 Usually no one will hurt you for wanting to do good.

14 But even if they should, you are to be envied, for God will reward you for it.

15 Quietly trust yourself to Christ your Lord and if anybody asks why you believe as you do, be ready to tell him, and do it in a gentle and respectful way.

16 Do what is right; then if men speak against you, calling you evil names, they will become ashamed of themselves for falsely accusing you when you have only done what is good.

17 Remember, if God wants you to suffer, it is better to suffer for doing good than for doing wrong!

18 Christ also suffered. . .

∽ 14 ∽

When You Feel Impatient

How you can develop patience

GALATIANS 5

22 But when the Holy Spirit controls our lives he will produce this kind of fruit in us: love, joy, peace, patience, kindness, goodness, faithfulness,

23 gentleness and self-control; and here there is no conflict with Jewish laws.

25 If we are living now by the Holy Spirit's power, let us follow the Holy Spirit's leading in every part of our lives.

ROMANS 5

3 We can rejoice, too, when we run into problems and trials for we know that they are good for us—they help us learn to be patient.

4 And patience develops strength of character in us and helps us trust God more each time we use it until finally our hope and faith are strong and steady.

5 Then, when that happens, we are able to hold our heads high no matter what happens and know that all is well, for we know how dearly God loves us, and we feel this warm love everywhere within us because God has given us the Holy Spirit to fill our hearts with his love.

2 THESSALONIANS 3

5 May the Lord bring you into an ever deeper understanding of the love of God and of the patience that comes from Christ.

ISAIAH 26

2 Open the gates to everyone, for all may enter in who love the Lord.

3 He will keep in perfect peace all those who trust in him, whose thoughts turn often to the Lord!

4 Trust in the Lord God always, for in the Lord Jehovah is your everlasting strength.

ROMANS 8

25 But if we must keep trusting God for something that hasn't happened yet, it teaches us to wait patiently and confidently.

JAMES 1

2 Dear brothers, is your life full of difficulties and temptations? Then be happy,

3 For when the way is rough, your patience has a chance to grow.

4 So let it grow, and don't try to squirm out of your problems. For when your patience is finally in full bloom, then you will be ready for anything, strong in character, full and complete.

HEBREWS 12

1 Since we have such a huge crowd of men of faith watching us from the grandstands, let us strip off anything that slows us down or holds us back, and especially those sins that wrap themselves so tightly around our feet and trip us up; and let us run with patience the particular race that God has set before us.

2 Keep your eyes on Jesus, our leader and instructor. He was willing to die a shameful death on the cross because of the joy he

knew would be his afterwards; and now he sits in the place of honor by the throne of God.

3 If you want to keep from becoming fainthearted and weary, think about his patience as sinful men did such terrible things to him.

4 After all, you have never yet struggled against sin and temptation until you sweat great drops of blood.

REVELATION 1

9 It is I, your brother John, a fellow sufferer for the Lord's sake, who am writing this letter to you. I, too, have shared the patience Jesus gives, and we shall share his kingdom!

2 PETER 1

6 Next, learn to put aside your own desires so that you will become patient and godly, gladly letting God have his way with you.

Waiting and trusting

PSALM 40

1 I waited patiently for God to help me; then he listened and heard my cry.

2 He lifted me out of the pit of despair, out from the bog and the mire, and set my feet on a hard, firm path and steadied me as I walked along.

3 He has given me a new song to sing, of praises to our God. Now many will hear of the glorious things he did for me, and stand in awe before the Lord, and put their trust in him.

4 Many blessings are given to those who trust the Lord, and have no confidence in those who are proud, or who trust in idols.

5 O Lord my God, many and many a time you have done great miracles for us, and we are ever in your thoughts. Who else can do such glorious things? No one else can be compared with you. There isn't time to tell of all your wonderful deeds.

God is not hurried or harried

PSALM 90

1 Lord, through all the generations you have been our home!

2 Before the mountains were created, before the earth was formed, you are God without beginning or end.

3 You speak, and man turns back to dust.

4 A thousand years are but as yesterday to you! They are like a single hour!

5,6 We glide along the tides of time as swiftly as a racing river, and vanish as quickly as a dream. We are like grass that is green in the morning but mowed down and withered before the evening shadows fall.

PSALM 37

34 Don't be impatient for the Lord to act! Keep traveling steadily along his pathway and in due season he will honor you with every blessing, and you will see the wicked destroyed.

35 I myself have seen it happen.

∽ 15 ∽

When You Feel Lazy

The Proverbs talk about laziness

PROVERBS 25

13 A faithful employee is as refreshing as a cool day in the hot summertime.

PROVERBS 24

30,31 I walked by the field of a certain lazy fellow and saw that it was overgrown with thorns, and covered with weeds; and its walls were broken down.

32,33 Then, as I looked, I learned this lesson:
"A little extra sleep,
A little more slumber,
A little folding of the hands to rest"

34 Means that poverty will break in upon you suddenly like a robber, and violently like a bandit.

PROVERBS 21

25,26 The lazy man longs for many things but his hands refuse to work. He is greedy to get, while the godly love to give!

PROVERBS 18

9 A lazy man is brother to the saboteur.

PROVERBS 10

4 Lazy men are soon poor; hard workers get rich.

5 A wise youth makes hay while the sun shines, but what a shame to see a lad who sleeps away his hour of opportunity.

26 A lazy fellow is a pain to his employers—like smoke in their eyes or vinegar that sets the teeth on edge.

PROVERBS 16

26 Hunger is good—if it makes you work to satisfy it!

27 Idle hands are the devil's workshop; idle lips are his mouthpiece.

PROVERBS 6

6 Take a lesson from the ants, you lazy fellow. Learn from their ways and be wise!

7 For though they have no king to make them work,

8 Yet they labor hard all summer, gathering food for the winter.

9 But you—all you do is sleep. When will you wake up?

10 "Let me sleep a little longer!" Sure, just a little more!

11 And as you sleep, poverty creeps upon you like a robber and destroys you; want attacks you in full armor.

PROVERBS 13

4 Lazy people want much but get little, while the diligent are prospering.

PROVERBS 20

4 If you won't plow in the cold, you won't eat at the harvest.

13 If you love sleep, you will end in poverty. Stay awake, work hard, and there will be plenty to eat!

PROVERBS 22

29 Do you know a hard-working man? He shall be successful and stand before kings!

PROVERBS 26

10 The master may get better work from an untrained apprentice than from a skilled rebel!

11 As a dog returns to his vomit, so a fool repeats his folly.

12 There is one thing worse than a fool, and that is a man who is conceited.

13 The lazy man won't go out and work. "There might be a lion outside!" he says.

14 He sticks to his bed like a door to its hinges!

15 He is too tired even to lift his food from his dish to his mouth!

16 Yet in his own opinion he is smarter than seven wise men.

PROVERBS 12

11 Hard work means prosperity; only a fool idles away his time.

24 Work hard and become a leader; be lazy and never succeed.

27 A lazy man won't even dress the game he gets while hunting, but the diligent man makes good use of everything he finds.

PROVERBS 15

19 A lazy fellow has trouble all through life; the good man's path is easy!

* * *

Colossians 3

23 Work hard and cheerfully at all you do, just as though you were working for the Lord and not merely for your masters,

24 Remembering that it is the Lord Christ who is going to pay you, giving you your full portion of all he owns. He is the one you are really working for.

25 And if you don't do your best for him, he will pay you in a way that you won't like—for he has no special favorites who can get away with shirking.

Romans 12

11 Never be lazy in your work but serve the Lord enthusiastically.

1 Timothy 5

18 For the Scriptures say, "Never tie up the mouth of an ox when it is treading out the grain—let him eat as he goes along!" And in another place, "Those who work deserve their pay!"

2 Thessalonians 3

6 Now here is a command, dear brothers, given in the name of our Lord Jesus Christ by his authority: Stay away from any Christian who spends his days in laziness and does not follow the ideal of hard work we set up for you.

7 For you well know that you ought to follow our example: you never saw us loafing;

8 We never accepted food from anyone without buying it; we worked hard day and night for the money we needed to live on, in order that we would not be a burden to any of you.

9 It wasn't that we didn't have the right to ask you to feed us, but we wanted to show you, firsthand, how you should work for your living.

10 Even while we were still there with you we gave you this rule: "He who does not work shall not eat."

11 Yet we hear that some of you are living in laziness, refusing to work, and wasting your time in gossiping.

12 In the name of the Lord Jesus Christ we appeal to such people—we command them—to quiet down, get to work, and earn their own living.

~16~

When You Feel Life Is Meaningless, Without Purpose

Why you are on earth

Acts 17

26 He created all the people of the world from one man, Adam, and scattered the nations across the face of the earth. He decided beforehand which should rise and fall, and when. He determined their boundaries.

27 His purpose in all of this is that they should seek after God, and perhaps feel their way toward him and find him—though he is not far from any one of us.

Ephesians 1

11 Moreover, because of what Christ has done we have become gifts to God that he delights in, for as part of God's sovereign plan we were chosen from the beginning to be his, and all things happen just as he decided long ago.

12 God's purpose in this was that we should praise God and give glory to him for doing these mighty things for us, who were the first to trust in Christ.

PHILIPPIANS 1

25 Yes, I am still needed down here and so I feel certain I will be staying on earth a little longer, to help you grow and become happy in your faith;

26 My staying will make you glad and give you reason to glorify Christ Jesus for keeping me safe, when I return to visit you again.

ISAIAH 43

7 All who claim me as their God will come, for I have made them for my glory; I created them.

HEBREWS 6

11 And we are anxious that you keep right on loving others as long as life lasts, so that you will get your full reward.

12 Then, knowing what lies ahead for you, you won't become bored with being a Christian, nor become spiritually dull and indifferent, but you will be anxious to follow the example of those who receive all that God has promised them because of their strong faith and patience.

Your purpose in life is to love

MARK 12

28 One of the teachers of religion who was standing there listening to the discussion realized that Jesus had answered well. So he asked, "Of all the commandments, which is the most important?"

29 Jesus replied, "The one that says, 'Hear, O Israel! The Lord our God is the one and only God.

30 And you must love him with all your heart and soul and mind and strength.'

31 The second is: 'You must love others as much as yourself.' No other commandments are greater than these."

MATTHEW 5

43 There is a saying, 'Love your *friends* and hate your enemies.'

44 But I say: Love your *enemies!* Pray for those who *persecute* you!

45 In that way you will be acting as true sons of your Father in heaven. For he gives his sunlight to both the evil and the good, and sends rain on the just and on the unjust too.

46 If you love only those who love you, what good is that? Even scoundrels do that much.

47 If you are friendly only to your friends, how are you different from anyone else? Even the heathen do that.

48 But you are to be perfect, even as your Father in heaven is perfect.

EPHESIANS 2

10 It is God himself who has made us what we are and given us new lives from Christ Jesus; and long ages ago he planned that we should spend these lives in helping others.

Your purpose in life is to follow Christ

MARK 8

34 Then he called his disciples and the crowds to come over and listen. "If any of you wants to be my follower," he told them, "you must put aside your own pleasures and shoulder your cross, and follow me closely.

35 If you insist on saving your life, you will lose it. Only those who throw away their lives for my sake and for the sake of the Good News will ever know what it means to really live.

2 CORINTHIANS 5

9 So our aim is to please him always in everything we do, whether we are here in this body or away from this body and with him in heaven.

95

15 He died for all so that all who live--having received eternal life from him—might live no longer for themselves, to please themselves, but to spend their lives pleasing Christ who died and rose again for them.

Your purpose in life is to do God's will

JOHN 4

34 Then Jesus explained: "My nourishment comes from doing the will of God who sent me, and from finishing his work.

35 Do you think the work of harvesting will not begin until the summer ends four months from now? Look around you! Vast fields of human souls are ripening all around us, and are ready now for reaping.

36 The reapers will be paid good wages and will be gathering eternal souls into the granaries of heaven! What joys await the sower and the reaper, both together!"

Your purpose in life is to spread the Word

EPHESIANS 3

1 I Paul, the servant of Christ, am here in jail because of you—for preaching that you Gentiles are a part of God's house.

2,3 No doubt you already know that God has given me this special work of showing God's favor to you Gentiles, as I briefly mentioned before in one of my letters. God himself showed me this secret plan of his, that the Gentiles, too, are included in his kindness.

7 God has given me the wonderful privilege of telling everyone about this plan of his; and he has given me his power and special ability to do it well.

2 Corinthians 4

1 It is God himself, in his mercy, who has given us this wonderful work [of telling his Good News to others], and so we never give up.

5 We don't go around preaching about ourselves, but about Christ Jesus as Lord. All we say of ourselves is that we are your slaves because of what Jesus has done for us.

6 For God, who said, "Let there be light in the darkness," has made us understand that it is the brightness of his glory that is seen in the face of Jesus Christ.

Your purpose in life is to live for God

1 Thessalonians 4

1 Let me add this, dear brothers: You already know how to please God in your daily living, for you know the commands we gave you from the Lord Jesus himself. Now we beg you—yes, we demand of you in the name of the Lord Jesus—that you live more and more closely to that ideal.

3,4 For God wants you to be holy and pure, and to keep clear of all sexual sin so that each of you will marry in holiness and honor—

5 Not in lustful passion as the heathen do, in their ignorance of God and his ways.

6 And this also is God's will: that you never cheat in this matter by taking another man's wife, because the Lord will punish you terribly for this, as we have solemnly told you before.

7 For God has not called us to be dirty-minded and full of lust, but to be holy and clean.

8 If anyone refuses to live by these rules he is not disobeying the rules of men but of God who gives his *Holy* Spirit to you.

9 But concerning the pure brotherly love that there should be among God's people, I don't need to say very much, I'm sure! For God himself is teaching you to love one another.

10 Indeed, your love is already strong toward all the Christian brothers throughout your whole nation. Even so, dear friends, we beg you to love them more and more.

11 This should be your ambition: to live a quiet life, minding your own business and doing your own work, just as we told you before.

12 As a result, people who are not Christians will trust and respect you, and you will not need to depend on others for enough money to pay your bills.

1 JOHN 2

16 For all these worldly things, these evil desires—the craze for sex, the ambition to buy everything that appeals to you, and the pride that comes from wealth and importance—these are not from God. They are from this evil world itself.

17 And this world is fading away, and these evil, forbidden things will go with it, but whoever keeps doing the will of God will live forever.

28 And now, my little children, stay in happy fellowship with the Lord so that when he comes you will be sure that all is well, and will not have to be ashamed and shrink back from meeting him.

29 Since we know that God is always good and does only right, we may rightly assume that all those who do right are his children.

What God wants of you
God wants you to trust Him, to obey Him

PROVERBS 22

17,18,19 Listen to this wise advice; follow it closely, for it will do you good, and you can pass it on to others: *Trust in the Lord.*

PROVERBS 16

20 God blesses those who obey him; happy the man who puts his trust in the Lord.

JEREMIAH 7

21 The Lord of Hosts, the God of Israel says, Away with your offerings and sacrifices!

22 It wasn't offerings and sacrifices I wanted from your fathers when I led them out of Egypt. That was not the point of my command.

23 But what I told them was: *Obey* me and I will be your God and you shall be my people; only do as I say and all shall be well!

AMOS 5

21 I hate your show and pretense—your hypocrisy of 'honoring' me with your religious feasts and solemn assemblies.

22 I will not accept your burnt offerings and thank offerings. I will not look at your offerings of peace.

23 Away with your hymns of praise—they are mere noise to my ears. I will not listen to your music, no matter how lovely it is.

24 I want to see a mighty flood of justice—a torrent of doing good.

PROVERBS 2

20 Follow the steps of the godly instead, and stay on the right path.

21 For only good men enjoy life to the full;

22 Evil men lose the good things they might have had, and they themselves shall be destroyed.

1 PETER 1

14 Obey God because you are his children; don't slip back into your old ways—doing evil because you knew no better.

15 But be holy now in everything you do, just as the Lord is holy, who invited you to be his child.

16 He himself has said, "You must be holy, for I am holy."

17 And remember that your heavenly Father to whom you pray has no favorites when he judges. He will judge you with perfect justice for everything you do; so act in reverent fear of him from now on until you get to heaven.

18 God paid a ransom to save you from the impossible road to heaven which your fathers tried to take, and the ransom he paid was not mere gold or silver, as you very well know.

19 But he paid for you with the precious lifeblood of Christ, the sinless, spotless Lamb of God.

20 God chose him for this purpose long before the world began, but only recently was he brought into public view, in these last days, as a blessing to you.

21 Because of this, your trust can be in God who raised Christ from the dead and gave him great glory. Now your faith and hope can rest in him alone.

22 Now you can have real love for everyone because your souls have been cleansed from selfishness and hatred when you trusted Christ to save you; so see to it that you really do love each other warmly, with all your hearts.

23 For you have a new life. It was not passed on to you from your parents, for the life they gave you will fade away. This new one will last forever, for it comes from Christ, God's ever-living Message to men.

24 Yes, our natural lives will fade as grass does when it becomes all brown and dry. All our greatness is like a flower that droops and falls;

25 But the Word of the Lord will last forever. And his message is the Good News that was preached to you.

HEBREWS 13

15 With Jesus' help we will continually offer our sacrifice of praise to God by telling others of the glory of his name.

16 Don't forget to do good and to share what you have with those in need, for such sacrifices are very pleasing to him.

JEREMIAH 17

5 The Lord says: Cursed is the man who puts his trust in mortal man and turns his heart away from God.

6 He is like a stunted shrub in the desert, with no hope for the future; he lives on the salt-encrusted plains in the barren wilderness; good times pass him by forever.

7 But blessed is the man who trusts in the Lord and has made the Lord his hope and confidence.

8 He is like a tree planted along a riverbank, with its roots reaching deep into the water—a tree not bothered by the heat nor worried by long months of drought. Its leaves stay green and it goes right on producing all its luscious fruit.

REVELATION 1

6b ... Give to him everlasting glory! He rules forever! Amen!

REVELATION 2

4 Yet there is one thing wrong; you don't love me as at first!

5 Think about those times of your first love (how different now!) and turn back to me again and work as you did before ...

2 CORINTHIANS 13

9 We are glad to be weak and despised if you are really strong. Our greatest wish and prayer is that you will become mature Christians.

MARK 9

30,31 Leaving that region they traveled through Galilee where he tried to avoid all publicity in order to spend more time with his disciples, teaching them. He would say to them, "I, the Messiah, am going to be betrayed and killed and three days later I will return to life again."

32 But they didn't understand and were afraid to ask him what he meant.

33 And so they arrived at Capernaum. When they were settled in the house where they were to stay he asked them, "What were you discussing out on the road?"

34 But they were ashamed to answer, for they had been arguing about which of them was the greatest!

35 He sat down and called them around him and said, "Anyone wanting to be the greatest must be the least—the servant of all!"

36 Then he placed a little child among them; and taking the child in his arms he said to them,

37 "Anyone who welcomes a little child like this in my name is welcoming me, and anyone who welcomes me is welcoming my Father who sent me!"

PHILIPPIANS 2

3 Don't be selfish; don't live to make a good impression on others. Be humble, thinking of others as better than yourself.

4 Don't just think about your own affairs, but be interested in others, too, and in what they are doing.

5 Your attitude should be the kind that was shown us by Jesus Christ,

6 Who, though he was God, did not demand and cling to his rights as God,

7 But laid aside his mighty power and glory, taking the disguise of a slave and becoming like men.

8 And he humbled himself even further, going so far as actually to die a criminal's death on a cross.

9 Yet it was because of this that God raised him up to the heights of heaven and gave him a name which is above every other name,

10 That at the name of Jesus every knee shall bow in heaven and on earth and under the earth,

11 And every tongue shall confess that Jesus Christ is Lord, to the glory of God the Father.

❧ 17 ❧

When You Feel Your Problems Are Too Big For God

You can trust God

JEREMIAH 32

27 I am the Lord, the God of all mankind; is there anything too hard for me?

ISAIAH 48

12 Listen to me, my people, my chosen ones! I alone am God. I am the First; I am the Last.

13 It was my hand that laid the foundations of the earth; the palm of my right hand spread out the heavens above; I spoke and they came into being.

PSALM 37

39 The Lord saves the godly! He is their salvation and their refuge when trouble comes.

40 Because they trust in him, he helps them and delivers them from the plots of evil men.

1 Corinthians 2

9 That is what is meant by the Scriptures which say that no mere man has ever seen, heard or even imagined what wonderful things God has ready for those who love the Lord.

Isaiah 64

8 And yet, O Lord, you are our Father. We are the clay and you are the Potter. We are all formed by your hand.

Colossians 2

3 In him lie hidden all the mighty, untapped treasures of wisdom and knowledge.

Romans 11

33 Oh, what a wonderful God we have! How great are his wisdom and knowledge and riches! How impossible it is for us to understand his decisions and his methods!

34 For who among us can know the mind of the Lord? Who knows enough to be his counselor and guide?

35 And who could ever offer to the Lord enough to induce him to act?

36 For everything comes from God alone. Everything lives by his power, and everything is for his glory. To him be glory evermore.

Colossians 1

15 Christ is the exact likeness of the unseen God. He existed before God made anything at all, and, in fact,

16 And Christ himself is the Creator who made everything in heaven and earth, the things we can see and the things we can't; the spirit world with its kings and kingdoms, its rulers and authorities; all were made by Christ for his own use and glory.

17 He was before all else began and it is his power that holds everything together.

EPHESIANS 1

8 And he has showered down upon us the richness of his grace—for how well he understands us and knows what is best for us at all times.

ROMANS 8

28 And we know that all that happens to us is working for our good if we love God and are fitting into his plans.

PSALM 145

17 The Lord is fair in everything he does, and full of kindness.
18 He is close to all who call on him sincerely.
19 He fulfills the desires of those who reverence and trust him; he hears their cries for help and rescues them.
20 He protects all those who love him, but destroys the wicked.
21 I will praise the Lord and call on all men everywhere to bless his holy name forever and forever.

EPHESIANS 3

20 Now glory be to God who by his mighty power at work within us is able to do far more than we would ever dare to ask or even dream of—infinitely beyond our highest prayers, desires, thoughts, or hopes.

HABAKKUK 2

20 But the Lord is in his holy Temple; let all the earth be silent before him.

2 CHRONICLES 16

9 For the eyes of the Lord search back and forth across the whole earth, looking for people whose hearts are perfect toward him, so that he can show his great power in helping them.

PSALM 125

1 Those who trust in the Lord are steady as Mount Zion, unmoved by any circumstance.

JEREMIAH 29

11 For I know the plans I have for you, says the Lord. They are plans for good and not for evil, to give you a future and a hope.

12 In those days when you pray, I will listen.

13 You will find me when you seek me, if you look for me in earnest.

Your God is too small

PSALM 107

23 And then there are the sailors sailing the seven seas, plying the trade routes of the world.

24 They, too, observe the power of God in action.

25 He calls to the storm winds; the waves rise high.

26 Their ships are tossed to the heavens and sink again to the depths; the sailors cringe in terror.

27 They reel and stagger like drunkards and are at their wit's end.

28 Then they cry to the Lord in their trouble, and he saves them.

29 He calms the storm and stills the waves.

30 What a blessing is that stillness, as he brings them safely into harbor!

31 Oh, that these men would praise the Lord for his lovingkindness and for all of his wonderful deeds!

32 Let them praise him publicly before the congregation, and before the leaders of the nation.

33 He dries up rivers,

34 And turns the good land of the wicked into deserts of salt.

35 Again, he turns deserts into fertile, watered valleys.

36 He brings the hungry to settle there and build their cities,

37 To sow their fields and plant their vineyards, and reap their bumper crops!

38 How he blesses them! They raise big families there, and many cattle.

ACTS 17

24 He made the world and everything in it, and since he is Lord of heaven and earth, he doesn't live in man-made temples;

25 And human hands can't minister to his needs—for he has no needs! He himself gives life and breath to everything, and satisfies every need there is.

26 He created all the people of the world from one man, Adam, and scattered the nations across the face of the earth. He decided beforehand which should rise and fall, and when. He determined their boundaries.

27 His purpose in all of this is that they should seek after God, and perhaps feel their way toward him and find him—though he is not far from any one of us.

AMOS 4

12b ... Prepare to meet your God in judgment, Israel.

13 For you are dealing with the one who formed the mountains and made the winds, and knows your every thought; he turns the morning to darkness and crushes down the mountains underneath his feet: Jehovah, the Lord, the God of Hosts, is his name.

Amos 5

8 Seek him who created the Seven Stars and the constellation Orion, who turns darkness into morning, and day into night, who calls forth the water from the ocean and pours it out as rain upon the land. The Lord, Jehovah, is his name.

9 With blinding speed and violence he brings destruction on the strong breaking all defenses.

Proverbs 30

4 Who else but God goes back and forth to heaven? Who else holds the wind in his fists, and wraps up the oceans in his cloak? Who but God has created the world? If there is any other, what is his name—and his son's name—if you know it?

Psalm 104

1,2 I bless the Lord: O Lord my God, how great you are! You are robed with honor and with majesty and light! You stretched out the starry curtain of the heavens,

3 And hollowed out the surface of the earth to form the seas. The clouds are his chariots. He rides upon the wings of the wind.

4 The angels are his messengers--his servants of fire!

5 You bound the world together so that it would never fall apart.

6 You clothed the earth with floods of waters covering up the mountains.

7,8 You spoke, and at the sound of your shout the water collected into its vast ocean beds, and mountains rose and valleys sank to the levels you decreed.

9 And then you set a boundary for the seas, so that they would never again cover the earth.

10 He placed springs in the valleys, and streams that gush from the mountains.

11 They give water for all the animals to drink. There the wild donkeys quench their thirst.

12 And the birds nest beside the streams and sing among the branches of the trees.

13 He sends rain upon the mountains and fills the earth with fruit.

14 The tender grass grows up at his command to feed the cattle, and there are fruit trees, vegetables and grain for man to cultivate.

15 And wine to make him glad, and olive oil as lotion for his skin, and bread to give him strength.

16 The Lord planted the cedars of Lebanon. They are tall and flourishing.

17 There the birds make their nests, the storks in the firs.

18 High in the mountains are pastures for the wild goats, and rock-badgers burrow in among the rocks and find protection there.

19 He assigned the moon to mark the months, and the sun to mark the days.

20 He sends the night and darkness, when all the forest folk come out.

21 Then the young lions roar for their food, but they are dependent on the Lord.

22 At dawn they slink back into their dens to rest.

23 And men go off to work until the evening shadows fall again.

24 O Lord, what a variety you have made! And in wisdom you have made them all! The earth is full of your riches.

25 There before me lies the mighty ocean, teeming with life of every kind, both great and small.

26 And look! See the ships! And over there, the whale you made to play in the sea.

27 Every one of these depends on you to give them daily food.

28 You supply it, and they gather it. You open wide your hand to feed them and they are satisfied with all your bountiful provision.

29 But if you turn away from them, then all is lost. And when you gather up their breath, they die and turn again to dust.

30 Then you send your spirit, and new life is born to replenish all the living of the earth.

31 Praise God forever! How he must rejoice in all his work!

32 The earth trembles at his glance; the mountains burst into flame at his touch.

33 I will sing to the Lord as long as I live. I will praise God to my last breath!

34 May he be pleased by all these thoughts about him, for He is the source of all my joy.

35 Let all sinners perish—all who refuse to praise him. But I will praise him. Hallelulah!

PSALM 90

1 Lord, through all the generations you have been our home!

2 Before the mountains were created, before the earth was formed, you are God without beginning or end.

3 You speak, and man turns back to dust.

4 A thousand years are but as yesterday to you! They are like a single hour!

MARK 4

35 As evening fell, Jesus said to his disciples, "Let's cross to the other side of the lake."

36 So they took him just as he was and started out, leaving the crowds behind (though other boats followed).

37 But soon a terrible storm arose. High waves began to break into the boat until it was nearly full of water and about to sink.

38 Jesus was asleep at the back of the boat with his head on a cushion. Frantically they wakened him, shouting, "Teacher, don't you even care that we are all about to drown?"

39 Then he rebuked the wind and said to the sea, "Quiet down!" And the wind fell, and there was a great calm!

40 And he asked them, "Why were you so fearful? Don't you even yet have confidence in me?"

41 And they were filled with awe and said among themselves, "Who is this man, that even the winds and seas obey him?"

Have faith in God's power

ISAIAH 50

7 Because the Lord God helps me, I will not be dismayed; therefore, I have set my face like flint to do his will, and I know that I will triumph.

8 He who gives me justice is near. Who will dare to fight against me now? Where are my enemies? Let them appear!

9 See, the Lord God is for me! Who shall declare me guilty? All my enemies shall be destroyed like old clothes eaten up by moths!

ISAIAH 64

1 Oh, that you would burst forth from the skies and come down! How the mountains would quake in your presence!

2 The consuming fire of your glory would burn down the forests and boil the oceans dry. The nations would tremble before you; then your enemies would learn the reason for your fame!

3 So it was before when you came down, for you did awesome things beyond our highest expectations, and how the mountains quaked!

4 For since the world began no one has seen or heard of such a God as ours, who works for those who wait for him!

ISAIAH 40

10 Yes, the Lord God is coming with mighty power; he will rule with awesome strength. See, his reward is with him, to each as he has done.

11 He will feed his flock like a shepherd; he will carry the lambs in his arms and gently lead the ewes with young.

12 Who else has held the oceans in his hands and measured off the heavens with his ruler? Who else knows the weight of all the earth and weighs the mountains and the hills?

13 Who can advise the Spirit of the Lord or be his teacher or give him counsel?

17 All the nations are as nothing to him; in his eyes they are less than nothing—mere emptiness and froth.

18 How can we describe God? With what can we compare him?

22 It is God who sits above the circle of the earth. (The people below must seem to him like grasshoppers!) He is the one who stretches out the heavens like a curtain and makes his tent from them.

23 He dooms the great men of the world and brings them all to naught.

24 They hardly get started, barely take root, when he blows on them and their work withers and the wind carries them off like straw.

25 "With whom will you compare me? Who is my equal?" asks the Holy One.

26 Look up into the heavens! Who created all these stars? As a shepherd leads his sheep, calling each by its pet name, and counts them to see that none are lost or strayed, so God does with stars and planets!

∽ 18 ∽

When You Feel Proud, Boastful

Proverbs say a lot about pride

PROVERBS 16

5 Pride disgusts the Lord. Take my word for it— *proud men shall be punished.*
19 Better poor and humble than proud and rich.

PROVERBS 28

11 Rich men are conceited, but their real poverty is evident to the poor.

PROVERBS 27

1 Don't brag about your plans for tomorrow—wait and see what happens.
2 Don't praise yourself; let others do it!
21 The purity of silver and gold can be tested in a crucible, but a man is tested by his reaction to men's praise.

PROVERBS 29

23 Pride ends in a fall, while humility brings honor.

PROVERBS 30

32 If you have been a fool by being proud or plotting evil, don't brag about it—cover your mouth with your hand in shame.

PROVERBS 26

12 There is one thing worse than a fool, and that is a man who is conceited.

PROVERBS 25

27 Just as it is harmful to eat too much honey, so also it is bad for men to think about all the honors they deserve!

PROVERBS 17

19 Sinners love to fight; boasting is looking for trouble.

Boast only about how great God is

2 CORINTHIANS 12

1 This boasting is all so foolish, but let me go on. Let me tell about the visions I've had, and revelations from the Lord.

2,3 Fourteen years ago I was taken up to heaven for a visit. Don't ask me whether my body was there or just my spirit, for I don't know; only God can answer that. But anyway, there I was in paradise,

4 And heard things so astounding that they are beyond a man's power to describe or put in words (and anyway I am not allowed to tell them to others).

5 That experience is something worth bragging about, but I am not going to do it. I am going to boast only about how weak I am and how great God is to use such weakness for his glory.

6 I have plenty to boast about and would be no fool in doing it, but I don't want anyone to think more highly of me than he should

from what he can actually see in my life and my message.

Your attitude should be like Jesus'

PHILIPPIANS 2

3 Don't be selfish; don't live to make a good impression on others. Be humble, thinking of others as better than yourself.

4 Don't just think about your own affairs, but be interested in others, too, and in what they are doing.

5 Your attitude should be the kind that was shown us by Jesus Christ,

6 Who, though he was God, did not demand and cling to his rights as God,

7 But laid aside his mighty power and glory, taking the disguise of a slave and becoming like men.

8 And he humbled himself even further, going so far as actually to die a criminal's death on a cross.

9 Yet it was because of this that God raised him up to the heights of heaven and gave him a name which is above every other name,

10 That at the name of Jesus every knee shall bow in heaven and on earth and under the earth . . .

The kind of people God boasts about

MATTHEW 23

11 The more lowly your service to others, the greater you are. To be the greatest, be a servant.

12 But those who think themselves great shall be disappointed and humbled; and those who humble themselves shall be exalted.

1 CORINTHIANS 1

26 Notice among ourselves, dear brothers, that few of us who follow Christ have big names or power or wealth.

27 Instead, God has deliberately chosen to save those whom the world considers foolish and of little worth in order to shame those the world considers wise and great.

28 He has chosen the little people, those despised by the world, who just don't count for anything at all, and used them to bring down to nothing those the world considers great.

30 For it is from God alone that you have your life through Jesus Christ. He showed us God's plan of salvation; He was the one who made us acceptable to God; He made us pure and holy and gave himself to purchase our salvation.

31 As it says in the Scriptures, "If anyone is going to boast, let him only boast of what the Lord has done."

MARK 10

31 But many people who seem to be important now will be the least important then; and many who are considered least here shall be greatest there.

Pride will be punished

PSALM 18

27 You deliver the humble but condemn the proud and haughty ones.

DANIEL 4

37 Now, I, Nebuchadnezzar, praise and glorify and honor the King of Heaven, the Judge of all, whose every act is right and good; for he is able to take those who walk proudly and push them into the dust!

Another place the Bible talks about pride

LUKE 14

7 When he noticed that all who came to the dinner were trying to sit near the head of the table, he gave them this advice:

8 "If you are invited to a wedding feast, don't always head for the best seat. For if someone more respected than you shows up,

9 The host will bring him over to where you are sitting and say, 'Let this man sit here instead.' And you, embarrassed, will have to take whatever seat is left at the foot of the table!

10 Do this instead—start at the foot; and when your host sees you he will come and say, 'Friend, we have a better place than this for you!' Thus you will be honored in front of all the other guests.

11 For everyone who tries to honor himself shall be humbled; and he who humbles himself shall be honored."

ᔐ19ᔐ

When You Feel Resentful

From the Book of Proverbs

PROVERBS 20

22 Don't repay evil for evil. Wait for the Lord to handle the matter.

PROVERBS 26

24,25,26 A man with hate in his heart may sound pleasant enough, but don't believe him; for he is cursing you in his heart. Though he pretends to be so kind, his hatred will finally come to light for all to see.

PROVERBS 29

1 The man who is often reproved but refuses to accept criticism will suddenly be broken and never have another chance.

26 Do you want justice? Don't fawn on the judge, but ask the Lord for it!

Other Scriptures about resentment

LUKE 6

27 Listen, all of you. Love your *enemies*. Do *good* to those who *hate* you.

118

28 Pray for the happiness of those who *curse* you; implore God's blessing on those who *hurt* you.

29 If someone slaps you on one cheek, let him slap the other too! If someone demands your coat, give him your shirt besides.

30 Give what you have to anyone who asks you for it; and when things are taken away from you, don't worry about getting them back.

31 Treat others as you want them to treat you.

32 Do you think you deserve credit for merely loving those who love you? Even the godless do that!

33 And if you do good only to those who do you good—is that so wonderful? Even sinners do that much!

34 And if you lend money only to those who can repay you, what good is that? Even the most wicked will lend to their own kind for full return!

35 Love your *enemies!* Do good to *them!* Lend to *them!* And don't be concerned about the fact that they won't repay. Then your reward from heaven will be very great, and you will truly be acting as sons of God: for he is kind to the *unthankful* and to those who are *very wicked.*

36 Try to show as much compassion as your Father does.

MATTHEW 18

21 Then Peter came to him and asked, "Sir, how often should I forgive a brother who sins against me? Seven times?"

22 "No!" Jesus replied, "seventy times seven!"

MATTHEW 5

46 If you love only those who love you, what good is that? Even scoundrels do that much.

47 If you are friendly only to your friends, how are you different from anyone else? Even the heathen do that.

48 But you are to be perfect, even as your Father in heaven is perfect.

1 Peter 3

9 Don't repay evil for evil. Don't snap back at those who say unkind things about you. Instead, pray for God's help for them, for we are to be kind to others, and God will bless us for it.

10 If you want a happy, good life, keep control of your tongue, and guard your lips from telling lies.

11 Turn away from evil and do good. Try to live in peace even if you must run after it to catch and hold it!

12 For the Lord is watching his children, listening to their prayers; but the Lord's face is hard against those who do evil.

2 Corinthians 5

10 For we must all stand before Christ to be judged and have our lives laid bare—before him. Each of us will receive whatever he deserves for the good or bad things he has done in his earthly body.

1 Thessalonians 5

15 See that no one pays back evil for evil, but always try to do good to each other and to everyone else.

~ 20 ~

When You Feel Restless, Uneasy, Without Peace

How to get inner peace

ROMANS 8

5 Those who let themselves be controlled by their lower natures live only to please themselves, but those who follow after the Holy Spirit find themselves doing those things that please God.

6 Following after the Holy Spirit leads to life and peace, but following after the old nature leads to death,

PHILIPPIANS 4

4 Always be full of joy in the Lord; I say it again, rejoice!

5 Let everyone see that you are unselfish and considerate in all you do. Remember that the Lord is coming soon.

6 Don't worry about anything; instead, pray about everything; tell God your needs and don't forget to thank him for his answers.

7 If you do this you will experience God's peace, which is far more wonderful than the human mind can understand. His peace will keep your thoughts and your hearts quiet and at rest as you trust in Christ Jesus.

8 And now, brothers, as I close this letter let me say this one more thing: Fix your thoughts on what is true and good and right. Think about things that are pure and lovely, and dwell on the fine, good things in others. Think about all you can praise God for and be glad about.

9 Keep putting into practice all you learned from me and saw me doing, and the God of peace will be with you.

ISAIAH 26

3 He will keep in perfect peace all those who trust in him, whose thoughts turn often to the Lord!
4 Trust in the Lord God always, for in the Lord Jehovah is your everlasting strength.

GALATIANS 5

16 I advise you to obey only the Holy Spirit's instructions. He will tell you where to go and what to do, and then you won't always be doing the wrong things your evil nature wants you to.
19 But when you follow your own wrong inclinations your lives will produce these evil results: impure thoughts, eagerness for lustful pleasure,
20 Idolatry, spiritism (that is, encouraging the activity of demons), hatred and fighting, jealousy and anger, constant effort to get the best for yourself, complaints and criticisms, the feeling that everyone else is wrong except those in your own little group—and there will be wrong doctrine,
21 Envy, murder, drunkenness, wild parties, and all that sort of thing. Let me tell you again as I have before, that anyone living that sort of life will not inherit the kingdom of God.
22 But when the Holy Spirit controls our lives he will produce this kind of fruit in us: love, joy, peace, patience, kindness, goodness, faithfulness,
23 Gentleness and self-control; and here there is no conflict with Jewish laws.

JOHN 14

27 I am leaving you with a gift—peace of mind and heart! And the peace I give isn't fragile like the peace the world gives. So don't be troubled or afraid.

PROVERBS 1

33 But all who listen to me shall live in peace and safety, unafraid.

JEREMIAH 6

16 Yet the Lord pleads with you still: Ask where the good road is, the godly paths you used to walk in, in the days of long ago. Travel there, and you will find rest for your souls.

PROVERBS 10

10 Winking at sin leads to sorrow; bold reproof leads to peace.

ISAIAH 26

12 Lord, grant us peace; for all we have and are has come from you.

MATTHEW 11

28 Come to me and I will give you rest—all of you who work so hard beneath a heavy yoke.

29,30 Wear my yoke—for it fits perfectly—and let me teach you; for I am gentle and humble, and you shall find rest for your souls; for I give you only light burdens.

NUMBERS 6

24,25,26 May the Lord bless and protect you; may the Lord's face radiate with joy because of you; may he be gracious to you, show you his favor, and give you his peace.

ISAIAH 57

15 The high and lofty one who inhabits eternity, the Holy One, says this: I live in that high and holy place where those with contrite, humble spirits dwell; and I refresh the humble and give new courage to those with repentant hearts.

18 I have seen what they do, but I will heal them anyway! I will lead them and comfort them, helping them to mourn and to confess their sins.

19 Peace, peace to them, both near and far, for I will heal them all.

20 But those who still reject me are like the restless sea, which is never still, but always churns up mire and dirt.

21 There is no peace, says my God, for them!

PROVERBS 28

1 The wicked flee when no one is chasing them! But the godly are bold as lions!

Help and guidance for a peace-filled life

PSALM 23

1 Because the Lord is my Shepherd, I have everything I need!

2,3 He lets me rest in the meadow grass and leads me beside the quiet streams. He restores my failing health. He helps me do what honors him the most.

4 Even when walking through the dark valley of death I will not be afraid, for you are close beside me, guarding, guiding all the way.

5 You provide delicious food for me in the presence of my enemies. You have welcomed me as your guest; blessings overflow!

6 Your goodness and unfailing kindness shall be with me all of my life, and afterwards I will live with you forever in your home.

PSALM 91

1 We live within the shadow of the Almighty, sheltered by the God who is above all gods.

2 This I declare, that he alone is my refuge, my place of safety; he is my God, and I am trusting him.

4 He will shield you with his wings! They will shelter you. His faithful promises are your armor.

PSALM 73

23b . . . You are holding my right hand!

24 You will keep on guiding me all my life with your wisdom and counsel; and afterwards receive me into the glories of heaven!

EPHESIANS 1

19 I pray that you will begin to understand how incredibly great his power is to help those who believe him. It is that same mighty power

20 That raised Christ from the dead and seated him in the place of honor at God's right hand in heaven . . .

ROMANS 8

31 What can we ever say to such wonderful things as these? If God is on our side, who can ever be against us?

32 Since he did not spare even his own Son for us but gave him up for us all, won't he also surely give us everything else?

EPHESIANS 4

3 Try always to be led along together by the Holy Spirit, and so be at peace with one another.

How to find peace with God

COLOSSIANS 1

20 It was through what his Son did that God cleared a path for everything to come to him—all things in heaven and on earth—for Christ's death on the cross has made peace with God for all by his blood.

HEBREWS 4

1 Although God's promise still stands—his promise that all may enter his place of rest—we ought to tremble with fear because some of you may be on the verge of failing to get there after all.

2 For this wonderful news—the message that God wants to save us—has been given to us just as it was to those who lived in the time of Moses. But it didn't do them any good because they didn't believe it. They didn't mix it with faith.

3 For only we who believe God can enter into his place of rest. He has said, "I have sworn in my anger that those who don't believe me will never get in," even though he has been ready and waiting for them since the world began.

9 So there is a full complete rest *still waiting* for the people of God.

10 Christ has already entered there. He is resting from his work, just as God did after the creation.

11 Let us do our best to go into that place of rest, too, being careful not to disobey God as the children of Israel did, thus failing to get in.

PSALM 4

3 The Lord has set apart the redeemed for Himself. Therefore He will listen to me and answer when I call to Him.

8 I will lie down in peace and sleep, for though I am alone, O Lord, you will keep me safe.

PSALM 85

8 I am listening carefully to all the Lord is saying—for he speaks peace to his people, his saints, if they will only stop their sinning.

How to find peace with other people

PROVERBS 16

7 When a man is trying to please God, God makes even his worst enemies to be at peace with him.

EPHESIANS 2

14 For Christ himself is our way of peace. He has made peace between us Jews and you Gentiles by making us all one family, breaking down the wall of contempt that used to separate us.

Instructions for living peacefully with others

ROMANS 12

12 Be glad for all God is planning for you. Be patient in trouble and prayerful always.

13 When God's children are in need, you be the one to help them out. And get into the habit of inviting guests home for dinner or if they need lodging, for the night.

14 If someone mistreats you because you are a Christian, don't curse him; pray that God will bless him.

15 When others are happy, be happy with them. If they are sad, share their sorrow.

16 Work happily together. Don't try to act big. Don't try to get into the good graces of important people, but enjoy the company of ordinary folks. And don't think you know it all!

17 Never pay back evil for evil. Do things in such a way that everyone can see you are honest clear through.

18 Don't quarrel with anyone. Be at peace with everyone, just as much as possible.

19 Dear friends, never avenge yourselves. Leave that to God, for He has said that He will repay those who deserve it. (Don't take the law into your own hands.)

20 Instead, feed your enemy if he is hungry. If he is thirsty give him something to drink and you will be "heaping coals of fire on his head." In other words, he will feel ashamed of himself for what he has done to you.

21 Don't let evil get the upper hand but conquer evil by doing good.

JAMES 3

17 But the wisdom that comes from heaven is first of all pure and full of quiet gentleness. Then it is peace-loving and courteous. It allows discussion and is willing to yield to others; it is full of mercy and good deeds. It is wholehearted and straightforward and sincere.

18 And those who are peacemakers will plant seeds of peace and reap a harvest of goodness.

Hope for peace in the future

MICAH 4

1 But in the last days Mount Zion will be the most renowned of all the mountains of the world, praised by all nations; people from all over the world will make pilgrimages there.

2 "Come," they will say to one another, "let us visit the mountain of the Lord, and see the Temple of the God of Israel; he will tell us what to do, and we will do it." For in those days the whole world will be ruled by the Lord from Jerusalem! He will issue his laws and announce his decrees from there.

3 He will arbitrate among the nations, and dictate to strong nations far away. They will beat their swords into plowshares and their spears into pruning-hooks; nations shall no longer fight each

other, for all war will end. There will be universal peace, and all the military academies and training camps will be closed down.

4 Everyone will live quietly in his own home in peace and prosperity, for there will be nothing to fear. The Lord himself has promised this.

∽ 21 ∽

When You Feel Sad

God knows and cares about your sadness

PSALM 139

1 O Lord, you have examined my heart and know everything about me.

2 You know when I sit or stand. When far away you know my every thought.

3 You chart the path ahead of me, and tell me where to stop and rest. Every moment, you know where I am.

4 You know what I am going to say before I even say it.

17,18 How precious it is, Lord, to realize that you are thinking about me constantly! I can't even count how many times a day your thoughts turn towards me. And when I waken in the morning, you are still thinking of me!

ISAIAH 53

2 In God's eyes he was like a tender green shoot, sprouting from a root in dry and sterile ground. But in our eyes there was no attractiveness at all, nothing to make us want him.

3 We despised him and rejected him—a man of sorrows, acquainted with bitterest grief. We turned our backs on him and looked the other way when he went by. He was despised and we didn't care.

4 Yet it was *our* grief he bore, *our* sorrows that weighed him down. And we thought his troubles were a punishment from God, for his *own* sins!

5 But he was wounded and bruised for *our* sins. He was chastised that we might have peace; he was lashed—and we were healed!

7 He was oppressed and he was afflicted, yet he never said a word. He was brought as a lamb to the slaughter; and as a sheep before her shearers is dumb, so he stood silent before the ones condemning him.

8 From prison and trial they led him away to his death. But who among the people of that day realized it was their sins that he was dying for—that he was suffering their punishment?

9 He was buried like a criminal in a rich man's grave; but he had done no wrong, and had never spoken an evil word.

10 Yet it was the Lord's good plan to bruise him and fill him with grief. But when his soul has been made an offering for sin, then he shall have a multitude of children, many heirs. He shall live again and God's program shall prosper in his hands.

LUKE 13

34 "O Jerusalem, Jerusalem! The city that murders the prophets. The city that stones those sent to help her. How often I have wanted to gather your children together even as a hen protects her brood under her wings, but you wouldn't let me.

35 And now—now your house is left desolate. And you will never again see me until you say, 'Welcome to him who comes in the name of the Lord.'"

HEBREWS 2

18 For since he himself has now been through suffering and temptation, he knows what it is like when we suffer and are tempted, and he is wonderfully able to help us.

Help and guidance when you feel sad

PSALM 31

24 So cheer up! Take courage if you are depending on the Lord.

HABAKKUK 3

17 Even though the fig trees are all destroyed, and there is neither blossom left nor fruit, and though the olive crops all fail, and the fields lie barren; even if the flocks die in the fields and the cattle barns are empty,

18 Yet I will rejoice in the Lord; I will be happy in the God of my salvation.

19 The Lord God is my Strength, and he will give me the speed of a deer and bring me safely over the mountains.

PSALM 42

11 But O my soul, don't be discouraged. Don't be upset. Expect God to act! For I know that I shall again have plenty of reason to praise him for all that he will do. He is my help! He is my God!

PSALM 43

5 O my soul, why be so gloomy and discouraged? Trust in God! I shall again praise him for his wondrous help; he will make me smile again, *for he is my God!*

ISAIAH 49

14 Yet they say, "My Lord deserted us; he has forgotten us."

15 Never! Can a mother forget her little child and not have love for her own son? Yet even if that should be, I will not forget you.

HOSEA 6

1 Come, let us return to the Lord; it is he who has torn us—he will heal us. He has wounded—he will bind us up.

2 In just a couple of days, or three at the most, he will set us on our feet again, to live in his kindness!

3 Oh, that we might know the Lord! Let us press on to know him, and he will respond to us as surely as the coming of dawn or the rain of early spring.

PSALM 147

1 Hallelujah! Yes, praise the Lord! How good it is to sing his praises! How delightful, and how right!

3 He heals the brokenhearted, binding up their wounds.

4 He counts the stars and calls them all by name.

5 How great he is! His power is absolute! His understanding is unlimited.

PHILIPPIANS 3

1 Whatever happens, dear friends, be glad in the Lord. I never get tired of telling you this and it is good for you to hear it again and again.

ROMANS 5

3 We can rejoice, too, when we run into problems and trials for we know that they are good for us—they help us learn to be patient.

2 CORINTHIANS 7

8 I am no longer sorry that I sent that letter to you, though I was very sorry for a time, realizing how painful it would be to you. But it hurt you only for a little while.

9 Now I am glad I sent it, not because it hurt you, but because the pain turned you to God. It was a good kind of sorrow you felt,

the kind of sorrow God wants his people to have, so that I need not come to you with harshness.

10 For God sometimes uses sorrow in our lives to help us turn away from sin and seek eternal life. We should never regret his sending it. But the sorrow of the man who is not a Christian is not the sorrow of true repentance and does not prevent eternal death.

Hope in times of sadness

ISAIAH 54

7 For a brief moment I abandoned you. But with great compassion I will gather you.

8 In a moment of anger I turned my face a little while; but with everlasting love I will have pity on you, says the Lord, your Redeemer.

ISAIAH 51

11 The time will come when God's redeemed will all come home again. They shall come with singing to Jerusalem, filled with joy and everlasting gladness; sorrow and mourning will all disappear.

12 I, even I, am he who comforts you and gives you all this joy. So what right have you to fear mere mortal men, who wither like the grass and disappear?

ISAIAH 40

25 "With whom will you compare me? Who is my equal?" asks the Holy One.

26 Look up into the heavens! Who created all these stars? As a shepherd leads his sheep, calling each by its pet name, and counts them to see that none are lost or strayed, so God does with stars and planets!

27 O Jacob, O Israel, how can you say that the Lord doesn't see your troubles and isn't being fair?

28 Don't you yet understand? Don't you know by now that the everlasting God, the Creator of the farthest parts of the earth, never grows faint or weary? No one can fathom the depths of his understanding.

29 He gives power to the tired and worn out, and strength to the weak.

30 Even the youths shall be exhausted, and the young men will all give up.

31 But they that wait upon the Lord shall renew their strength. They shall mount up with wings like eagles; they shall run and not be weary; they shall walk and not faint.

PSALM 102

17 He will listen to the prayers of the destitute, for he is never too busy to heed their requests.

PSALM 23

1 Because the Lord is my Shepherd, I have everything I need!

2,3 He lets me rest in the meadow grass and leads me beside the quiet streams. He restores my failing health. He helps me do what honors him the most.

4 Even when walking through the dark valley of death I will not be afraid, for you are close beside me, guarding, guiding all the way.

5 You provide delicious food for me in the presence of my enemies. You have welcomed me as your guest; blessings overflow!

6 Your goodness and unfailing kindness shall be with me all of my life, and afterwards I will live with you forever in your home.

2 THESSALONIANS 2

16 May our Lord Jesus Christ himself and God our Father, who has loved us and given us everlasting comfort and hope which we don't deserve,

17 Comfort your hearts with all comfort, and help you in every good thing you say and do.

PSALM 146

8 He opens the eyes of the blind; he lifts the burdens from those bent down beneath their loads. For the Lord loves good men.

PSALM 145

18 He is close to all who call on him sincerely.

19 He fulfills the desires of those who reverence and trust him; he hears their cries for help and rescues them.

LUKE 4

14 Then Jesus returned to Galilee, full of the Holy Spirit's power. Soon he became well known throughout all that region

15 For his sermons in the synagogues; everyone praised him.

16 When he came to the village of Nazareth, his boyhood home, he went as usual to the synagogue on Saturday, and stood up to read the Scriptures.

17 The book of Isaiah the prophet was handed to him, and he opened it to the place where it says:

18,19 The Spirit of the Lord is upon me; he has appointed me to preach Good News to the poor; he has sent me to heal the broken-hearted and to announce that captives shall be released and the blind shall see, that the downtrodden shall be freed from their oppressors, and that God is ready to give blessings to all who come to him."

20 He closed the book and handed it back to the attendant and sat down, while everyone in the synagogue gazed at him intently.

21 Then he added, "These Scriptures came true today!"

1 PETER 1

6 So be truly glad! There is wonderful joy ahead, even though the going is rough for a while down here.

1 PETER 5

10 After you have suffered a little while, our God, who is full of kindness through Christ, will give you his eternal glory. He personally will come and pick you up, and set you firmly in place, and make you stronger than ever.

11 To him be all power over all things, forever and ever. Amen.

2 PETER 3

13 But we are looking forward to God's promise of new heavens and a new earth afterwards, where there will be only goodness.

∽ 22 ∽

When You Feel Smarter,
Better Than Others

Death is a great equalizer of men

PSALM 49

10 Rich man! Proud man! Wise man! You must die like all the rest! You have no greater lease on life than foolish, stupid men. You must leave your wealth to others.

11 You name your estates after yourselves as though your lands could be forever yours, and you could live on them eternally.

12 But man with all his pomp must die like any animal.

13 Such is the folly of these men, though after they die they will be quoted as having great wisdom.

14 Death is the shepherd of all mankind. And "in the morning" those who are evil will be the slaves of those who are good. For the power of their wealth is gone when they die; they cannot take it with them.

15 But as for me, God will redeem my soul from the power of death, for he will receive me.

16 So do not be dismayed when evil men grow rich and build their lovely homes.

17 For when they die they carry nothing with them! Their honors will not follow them.

18 Though a man calls himself happy all through his life—and the world loudly applauds success—

19 Yet in the end he dies like everyone else, and enters eternal darkness.

Sin is a great equalizer of men

ROMANS 3

10 As the Scriptures say, "No one is good—no one in all the world is innocent."

11 No one has ever really followed God's paths, or even truly wanted to.

12 Every one has turned away; all have gone wrong. No one anywhere has kept on doing what is right; not one.

Reading God's Word is the answer

DEUTERONOMY 17

18 And when he has been crowned and sits upon his throne as king, then he must copy these laws from the book kept by the Levite-priests.

19 That copy of the laws shall be his constant companion. He must read from it every day of his life so that he will learn to respect the Lord his God by obeying all of his commands.

20 This regular reading of God's laws will prevent him from feeling that he is better than his fellow citizens. It will also prevent him from turning away from God's laws in the slightest respect, and will ensure his having a long, good reign.

God's criteria for greatness and wisdom

1 TIMOTHY 6

20 Keep out of foolish arguments with those who boast of their "knowledge" and thus prove their lack of it.

21 Some of these people have missed the most important thing in life—they don't know God. May God's mercy be upon you.

JEREMIAH 9

23 The Lord says: Let not the wise man bask in his wisdom, nor the mighty man in his might, nor the rich man in his riches.

24 Let them boast in this alone: That they truly know me, and understand that I am the Lord of justice and of righteousness whose love is steadfast; and that I love to be this way.

MARK 10

41 When the other disciples discovered what James and John had asked, they were very indignant.

42 So Jesus called them to him and said, "As you know, the kings and great men of the earth lord it over the people;

43 But among you it is different. Whoever wants to be great among you must be your servant.

44 And whoever wants to be greatest of all must be the slave of all.

45 For even I, the Messiah, am not here to be served, but to help others, and to give my life as a ransom for many."

PROVERBS 1

7 How does a man become wise? The first step is to trust and reverence the Lord!

COLOSSIANS 3

10 You are living a brand new kind of life that is continually learning more and more of what is right, and trying constantly to be more and more like Christ who created this new life within you.

11 In this new life one's nationality or race or education or social position is unimportant; such things mean nothing. Whether a person has Christ is what matters, and he is equally available to all.

Jesus deals with men who thought they were smarter than others

MATTHEW 18

1 About that time the disciples came to Jesus to ask which of them would be greatest in the Kingdom of Heaven!

2 Jesus called a small child over to him and set the little fellow down among them,

3 And said, "Unless you turn to God from your sins and become as little children, you will never get into the Kingdom of Heaven.

4 Therefore anyone who humbles himself as this little child, is the greatest in the Kingdom of Heaven.

5 And any of you who welcomes a little child like this because you are mine, is welcoming me and caring for me.

6 But if any of you causes one of these little ones who trusts in me to lose his faith, it would be better for you to have a rock tied to your neck and be thrown into the sea.

10 Beware that you don't look down upon a single one of these little children. For I tell you that in heaven their angels have constant access to my Father . . ."

MATTHEW 23

1 Then Jesus said to the crowds, and to his disciples,

2 "You would think these Jewish leaders and these Pharisees were Moses, the way they keep making up so many laws!

4 They load you with impossible demands that they themselves don't even try to keep.

5 Everything they do is done for show. They act holy by wearing on their arms little prayer boxes with Scripture verses inside, and by lengthening the memorial fringes of their robes.

6 And how they love to sit at the head table at banquets, and in the reserved pews in the synagogue!

7 How they enjoy the deference paid them on the streets, and to be called 'Rabbi' and 'Master'!"

11 The more lowly your service to others, the greater you are. To be the greatest, be a servant.

12 But those who think themselves great shall be disappointed and humbled; and those who humble themselves shall be exalted.

LUKE 18

9 Then he told this story to some who boasted of their virtue and scorned everyone else:

10 "Two men went to the Temple to pray. One was a proud, self-righteous Pharisee, and the other a cheating tax collector.

11 The proud Pharisee 'prayed' this prayer: 'Thank God, I am not a sinner like everyone else, especially like that tax collector over there! For I never cheat, I don't commit adultery,

12 I go without food twice a week, and I give to God a tenth of everything I earn.'

13 But the corrupt tax collector stood at a distance and dared not even lift his eyes to heaven as he prayed, but beat upon his chest in sorrow, exclaiming, 'God, be merciful to me, a sinner.'

14 I tell you, this sinner, not the Pharisee, returned home forgiven! For the proud shall be humbled, but the humble shall be honored."

Think about these!

PROVERBS 22

2 The rich and the poor are alike before the Lord who made them all.

DANIEL 4

35 All the people of the earth are nothing when compared to him; he does whatever he thinks best among the hosts of heaven, as well as here among the inhabitants of earth.

ROMANS 14

10 You have no right to criticize your brother or look down on him. Remember, each of us will stand personally before the Judgment Seat of God.

11 For it is written, "As I live," says the Lord, "every knee shall bow to me and every tongue confess to God."

12 Yes, each of us will give an account of himself to God.

ROMANS 12

15 When others are happy, be happy with them. If they are sad, share their sorrow.

16 Work happily together. Don't try to act big. Don't try to get into the good graces of important people, but enjoy the company of ordinary folks. And don't think you know it all!

ISAIAH 5

21 Woe to those who are wise and shrewd in their own eyes!

1 CORINTHIANS 3

18 Stop fooling yourselves. If you count yourself above average in intelligence, as judged by this world's standards, you had better put this all aside and be a fool rather than let it hold you back from the true wisdom from above.

19 For the wisdom of this world is foolishness to God. As it says in the book of Job, God uses man's own brilliance to trap him; he stumbles over his own "wisdom" and falls.

20 And again, in the book of Psalms, we are told that the Lord knows full well how the human mind reasons, and how foolish and futile it is.

PROVERBS 3

7,8 Don't be conceited, sure of your own wisdom. Instead, trust and reverence the Lord, and turn your back on evil; when you do that, then you will be given renewed health and vitality.

~ 23 ~

When You Feel Tempted

God is our strength

HEBREWS 4

13 He knows about everyone, everywhere. Everything about us is bare and wide open to the all-seeing eyes of our living God; nothing can be hidden from him to whom we must explain all that we have done.

14 But Jesus the Son of God is our great High Priest who has gone to heaven itself to help us; therefore let us never stop trusting him.

15 This High Priest of ours understands our weaknesses, since he had the same temptations we do, though he never once gave way to them and sinned.

16 So let us come boldly to the very throne of God and stay there to receive his mercy and to find grace to help us in our times of need.

1 CORINTHIANS 10

13 But remember this—the wrong desires that come into your life aren't anything new and different. Many others have faced exactly the same problems before you. And no temptation is irresistible. You can trust God to keep the temptation from becoming so strong that you can't stand up against it, for he has promised this and will do what he says. He will show you how to escape temptation's power so that you can bear up patiently against it.

PHILIPPIANS 1

6 And I am sure that God who began the good work within you will keep right on helping you grow in his grace until his task within you is finally finished on that day when Jesus Christ returns.

PSALM 32

7 You are my hiding place from every storm of life; you even keep me from getting into trouble! You surround me with songs of victory.

8 I will instruct you (says the Lord) and guide you along the best pathway for your life; I will advise you and watch your progress.

9 Don't be like a senseless horse or mule that has to have a bit in its mouth to keep it in line!

2 THESSALONIANS 3

2 Pray too that we will be saved out of the clutches of evil men, for not everyone loves the Lord.

3 But the Lord is faithful; he will make you strong and guard you from satanic attacks of every kind.

JUDE 1

24,25 And now—all glory to him who alone is God, who saves us through Jesus Christ our Lord; yes, splendor and majesty, all power and authority are his from the beginning; his they are and his they evermore shall be. And he is able to keep you from slipping and falling away, and to bring you, sinless and perfect, into his glorious presence with mighty shouts of everlasting joy. Amen.

2 CORINTHIANS 3

18b . . . And as the Spirit of the Lord works within us, we become more and more like him.

JAMES 4

5 Or what do you think the Scripture means when it says that the Holy Spirit, whom God has placed within us, watches over us with tender jealousy?

6 But he gives us more and more strength to stand against all such evil longings. . . .

1 CORINTHIANS 2

16b . . . But, strange as it seems, we Christians actually do have within us a portion of the very thoughts and mind of Christ.

2 PETER 2

9 So also the Lord can rescue you and me from the temptations that surround us, and continue to punish the ungodly until the day of final judgment comes.

1 CORINTHIANS 1

7 Now you have every grace and blessing; every spiritual gift and power for doing his will are yours during this time of waiting for the return of our Lord Jesus Christ.

Help in overcoming temptation

EPHESIANS 6

10 Last of all I want to remind you that your strength must come from the Lord's mighty power within you.

11 Put on all of God's armor so that you will be able to stand safe against all strategies and tricks of Satan.

12 For we are not fighting against people made of flesh and blood, but against persons without bodies—the evil rulers of the unseen world, those mighty satanic beings and great evil princes of darkness who rule this world; and against huge numbers of wicked spirits in the spirit world.

13 So use every piece of God's armor to resist the enemy whenever he attacks, and when it is all over, you will still be standing up.

14 But to do this, you will need the strong belt of truth and the breastplate of God's approval.

15 Wear shoes that are able to speed you on as you preach the Good News of peace with God.

16 In every battle you will need faith as your shield to stop the fiery arrows aimed at you by Satan.

17 And you will need the helmet of salvation and the sword of the Spirit—which is the Word of God.

18 Pray all the time. Ask God for anything in line with the Holy Spirit's wishes. Plead with him, reminding him of your needs, and keep praying earnestly for all Christians everywhere.

MATTHEW 26

41 Keep alert and pray. Otherwise temptation will overpower you. For the spirit indeed is willing, but how weak the body is!

PSALM 19

7,8 God's laws are perfect. They protect us, make us wise, and give us joy and light.

9 God's laws are pure, eternal, just.

10 They are more desirable than gold. They are sweeter than honey dripping from a honeycomb.

11 For they warn us away from harm and give success to those who obey them.

12 But how can I ever know what sins are lurking in my heart? Cleanse me from these hidden faults.

13 And keep me from deliberate wrongs; help me to stop doing them. Only then can I be free of guilt and innocent of some great crime.

14 May my spoken words and unspoken thoughts be pleasing even to you, O Lord my Rock and my Redeemer.

MATTHEW 6

9 Pray along these lines: 'Our Father in heaven, we honor your holy name.

10 We ask that your kingdom will come now. May your will be done here on earth, just as it is in heaven.

13 Don't bring us into temptation, but deliver us from the Evil One. Amen.'

PSALM 139

23 Search me, O God, and know my heart; test my thoughts.

24 Point out anything you find in me that makes you sad, and lead me along the path of everlasting life.

1 PETER 4

1 Since Christ suffered and underwent pain, you must have the same attitude he did; you must be ready to suffer, too. For remember, when your body suffers, sin loses its power,

2 And you won't be spending the rest of your life chasing after evil desires, but will be anxious to do the will of God.

GALATIANS 5

16 I advise you to obey only the Holy Spirit's instructions. He will tell you where to go and what to do, and then you won't always be doing the wrong things your evil nature wants you to.

17 For we naturally love to do evil things that are just the opposite from the things that the Holy Spirit tells us to do; and the good things we want to do when the Spirit has his way with us are just the opposite of our natural desires. These two forces within us are constantly fighting each other to win control over us, and our wishes are never free from their pressures.

Rewards for resisting temptation

MATTHEW 5

8 Happy are those whose hearts are pure, for they shall see God.

PSALM 17

15 But as for me, my contentment is not in wealth but in seeing you and knowing all is well between us. And when I awake in heaven, I will be fully satisfied, for I will see you face to face.

PSALM 15

1 Lord, who may go and find refuge and shelter in your tabernacle up on your holy hill?
2 Anyone who leads a blameless life and is truly sincere.
3 Anyone who refuses to slander others, does not listen to gossip, never harms his neighbor,
4 Speaks out against sin, criticizes those committing it, commends the faithful followers of the Lord, keeps a promise even if it ruins him,
5 Does not crush his debtors with high interest rates, and refuses to testify against the innocent despite the bribes offered him—such a man shall stand firm forever.

* * *

JEREMIAH 10

23 O Lord, I know it is not within the power of man to map his life and plan his course—
24 So you correct me, Lord; but please be gentle. Don't do it in your anger, for I would die.

~24~

When You Feel Thankful

Let's just praise the Lord!

PSALM 118

29 Oh, give thanks to the Lord, for he is so good! For his lovingkindness is forever.

PSALM 86

12 With all my heart I will praise you. I will give glory to your name forever,

13 For you love me so much! You are constantly so kind! You have rescued me from deepest hell.

PSALM 136

1 Oh, give thanks to the Lord, for he is good; his lovingkindness continues forever.

2 Give thanks to the God of gods, for his lovingkindness continues forever.

3 Give thanks to the Lord of lords, for his lovingkindness continues forever.

4 Praise him who alone does mighty miracles, for his lovingkindness continues forever.

5 Praise him who made the heavens, for his lovingkindness continues forever.

6 Praise him who planted the water within the earth, for his lovingkindness continues forever.

7 Praise him who made the heavenly lights, for his lovingkindness continues forever:

8 The sun to rule the day, for his lovingkindness continues forever;

9 And the moon and stars at night, for his lovingkindness continues forever.

10 Praise the God who smote the firstborn of Egypt, for his lovingkindness to Israel continues forever.

11,12 He brought them out with mighty power and upraised fist to strike their enemies, for his lovingkindness to Israel continues forever.

13 Praise the Lord who opened the Red Sea to make a path before them, for his lovingkindness continues forever,

14 And led them safely through, for his lovingkindness continues forever—

15 But drowned Pharaoh's army in the sea, for his lovingkindness to Israel continues forever.

16 Praise him who led his people through the wilderness, for his lovingkindness continues forever.

17 Praise him who saved his people from the power of mighty kings, for his lovingkindness continues forever,

23 He remembered our utter weakness, for his lovingkindness continues forever.

24 And saved us from our foes, for his lovingkindness continues forever.

25 He gives food to every living thing, for his lovingkindness continues forever.

26 Oh, give thanks to the God of heaven, for his lovingkindness continues forever.

PSALM 105

1 Thank the Lord for all the glorious things he does; proclaim them to the nations.

2 Sing his praises and tell everyone about his miracles.

3 Glory in the Lord; O worshipers of God, rejoice.

7 He is the Lord our God. His goodness is seen everywhere throughout the land.

PSALM 34

1 I will praise the Lord no matter what happens. I will constantly speak of his glories and grace.

2 I will boast of all his kindness to me. Let all who are discouraged take heart.

3 Let us praise the Lord together, and exalt his name.

PSALM 145

1,2 I will praise you, my God and King, and bless your name each day and forever.

3 Great is Jehovah! Greatly praise him! His greatness is beyond discovery!

4 Let each generation tell its children what glorious things he does.

5 I will meditate about your glory, splendor, majesty and miracles.

6 Your awe-inspiring deeds shall be on every tongue; I will proclaim your greatness.

7 Everyone will tell about how good you are, and sing about your righteousness.

8 Jehovah is kind and merciful, slow to get angry, full of love.

9 He is good to everyone, and his compassion is intertwined with everything he does.

10 All living things shall thank you, Lord, and your people will bless you.

11 They will talk together about the glory of your kingdom and mention examples of Your power.

12 They will tell about your miracles and about the majesty and glory of your reign.

13 For your kingdom never ends. You rule generation after generation.

14 The Lord lifts the fallen and those bent beneath their loads.

15 The eyes of all mankind look up to you for help; You give them their food as they need it.

16 You constantly satisfy the hunger and thirst of every living thing.

17 The Lord is fair in everything he does, and full of kindness.

18 He is close to all who call on him sincerely.

19 He fulfills the desires of those who reverence and trust him; he hears their cries for help and rescues them.

20 He protects all those who love him, but destroys the wicked.

21 I will praise the Lord and call on all men everywhere to bless his holy name forever and forever.

JAMES 5

13 And those who have reason to be thankful should continually be singing praises to the Lord.

Hallelujah!

PSALM 150

1 Hallelujah! Yes, praise the Lord!
Praise him in his Temple, and in the heavens he made with mighty power.

2 Praise him for his mighty works. Praise his unequaled greatness.

3 Praise him with the trumpet and with lute and harp.

4 Praise him with the tambourines and processional. Praise him with stringed instruments and horns.

5 Praise him with the cymbals, yes, loud clanging cymbals.

6 Let everything alive give praises to the Lord! *You* praise him! Hallelujah!

PSALM 149

1 Hallelujah! Yes, praise the Lord! Sing him a new song. Sing his praises, all his people.

2 O Israel, rejoice in your Maker. O people of Jerusalem, exult in your King.

3 Praise his name with dancing, accompanied by drums and lyre.

4,5 For Jehovah enjoys his people; he will save the humble. Let his people rejoice in this honor. Let them sing for joy as they lie upon their beds.

Sing His praises with music and harp

PSALM 92

1 It is good to say, "Thank you" to the Lord, to sing praises to the God who is above all gods.

2 Every morning tell him, "Thank you for your kindness," and every evening rejoice in all his faithfulness.

3 Sing his praises, accompanied by music from the harp and lute and lyre.

4 You have done so much for me, O Lord. No wonder I am glad! I sing for joy.

5 O Lord, what miracles you do! And how deep are your thoughts!

6 Unthinking people do not understand them! No fool can comprehend this:

7 that although the wicked flourish like weeds, there is only eternal destruction ahead of them.

8 But the Lord continues forever, exalted in the heavens,

9 While his enemies—all evil-doers—shall be scattered.

10 But you have made me as strong as a wild bull. How refreshed I am by your blessings!

11 I have heard the doom of my enemies announced and seen them destroyed.

12 But the godly shall flourish like palm trees, and grow tall as the cedars of Lebanon.

13 For they are transplanted into the Lord's own garden, and are under his personal care.

14 Even in old age they will still produce fruit and be vital and green.

15 This honors the Lord, and exhibits his faithful care. He is my shelter. There is nothing but goodness in him!

How Jonah thanked God

JONAH 2

5 I sank beneath the waves, and death was very near. The waters closed above me; the seaweed wrapped itself around my head.

6 I went down to the bottoms of the mountains that rise from off the ocean floor. I was locked out of life and imprisoned in the land of death. But, O Lord my God, you have snatched me from the yawning jaws of death!

7 When I had lost all hope, I turned my thoughts once more to the Lord. And my earnest prayer went to you in your holy Temple.

9 I will never worship anyone but you! For how can I thank you enough for all you have done? I will surely fulfill my promises.

If you are thankful, speak out!

PSALM 107

1 Say "Thank you" to the Lord for being so good, for always being so loving and kind.

2 Has the Lord redeemed you? Then speak out! Tell others he has saved you from your enemies.

43 Listen, if you are wise, to what I am saying. Think about the lovingkindness of the Lord!

~25~

When You Feel Unloved

See how God loves you!

MATTHEW 10

29 Not one sparrow (What do they cost? Two for a penny?) can fall to the ground without your Father knowing it.

30 And the very hairs of your head are all numbered.

31 So don't worry! You are more valuable to him than many sparrows.

1 JOHN 4

9 God showed how much he loved us by sending his only Son into this wicked world to bring to us eternal life through his death

10 In this act we see what real love is: it is not our love for God, but his love for us when he sent his Son to satisfy God's anger against our sins.

11 Dear friends, since God loved us as much as that, we surely ought to love each other too.

12 For though we have never yet seen God, when we love each other God lives in us and his love within us grows ever stronger.

13 And he has put his own Holy Spirit into our hearts as a proof to us that we are living with him and he with us.

14 And furthermore, we have seen with our own eyes and now tell all the world that God sent his Son to be their Savior.

15 Anyone who believes and says that Jesus is the Son of God has God living in him, and he is living with God.

16 We know how much God loves us because we have felt his love and because we believe him when he tells us that he loves us dearly. God is love, and anyone who lives in love is living with God and God is living in him.

17 And as we live with Christ, our love grows more perfect and complete; so we will not be ashamed and embarrassed at the day of judgment, but can face him with confidence and joy, because he loves us and we love him too.

18 We need have no fear of someone who loves us perfectly; his perfect love for us eliminates all dread of what he might do to us. If we are afraid, it is for fear of what he might do to us, and shows that we are not fully convinced that he really loves us.

19 So you see, our love for him comes as a result of his loving us first.

20 If anyone says "I love God," but keeps on hating his brother, he is a liar; for if he doesn't love his brother who is right there in front of him, how can he love God whom he has never seen?

21 And God himself has said that one must love not only God, but his brother too.

John 3

15 So that anyone who believes in me will have eternal life.

16 For God loved the world so much that he gave his only Son so that anyone who believes in him shall not perish but have eternal life.

17 God did not send his Son into the world to condemn it, but to save it.

Isaiah 43

1b . . . Don't be afraid, for I have ransomed you; I have called you by name; you are mine.

2 When you go through deep waters and great trouble, I will be with you. When you go through rivers of difficulty, you will not drown! When you walk through the fire of oppression, you will not be burned up—the flames will not consume you.

3 For I am the Lord your God, your Savior, the Holy One of Israel.

ROMANS 8

29 For from the very beginning God decided that those who came to him—and all along he knew who would—should become like his Son, so that his Son would be the First, with many brothers.

30 And having chosen us, he called us to come to him; and when we came, he declared us "not guilty," filled us with Christ's goodness, gave us right standing with himself, and promised us his glory.

31 What can we ever say to such wonderful things as these? If God is on our side, who can ever be against us?

32 Since he did not spare even his own Son for us but gave him up for us all, won't he also surely give us everything else?

REVELATION 1

5b . . . All praise to him who always loves us and who set us free from our sins by pouring out his lifeblood for us.

JOHN 16

27 for the Father himself loves you dearly because you love me and believe that I came from the Father.

EPHESIANS 3

17b . . . May your roots go down deep into the soil of God's marvelous love;

18,19 and may you be able to feel and understand, as all God's children should, how long, how wide, how deep, and how high his love really is; and to experience this love for yourselves, though it is so great that you will never see the end of it or fully know or understand it. And so at last you will be filled up with God himself.

ROMANS 5

8 But God showed his great love for us by sending Christ to die for us while we were still sinners.

1 CORINTHIANS 2

9b ... No mere man has ever seen, heard or even imagined what wonderful things God has ready for those who love the Lord.

EPHESIANS 2

1 Once you were under God's curse, doomed forever for your sins.

2 You went along with the crowd and were just like all the others, full of sin, obeying Satan, the mighty prince of the power of the air, who is at work right now in the hearts of those who are against the Lord.

3 All of us used to be just as they are, our lives expressing the evil within us, doing every wicked thing that our passions or our evil thoughts might lead us into. We started out bad, being born with evil natures, and were under God's anger just like everyone else.

4 But God is so rich in mercy; he loved us so much

5 That even though we were spiritually dead and doomed by our sins, he gave us back our lives again when he raised Christ from the dead—only by his undeserved favor have we ever been saved—

6 And lifted us up from the grave into glory along with Christ, where we sit with him in the heavenly realms—all because of what Christ Jesus did.

7 And now God can always point to us as examples of how very, very rich his kindness is, as shown in all he has done for us through Jesus Christ.

ZEPHANIAH 3

17,18 For the Lord your God has arrived to live among you. He is a mighty Savior. He will give you victory. He will rejoice over you in great gladness; he will love you and not accuse you." Is that a joyous choir I hear? No, it is the Lord himself exulting over you in happy song.

Believers are God's loved sons

1 JOHN 3

1 See how very much our heavenly Father loves us, for he allows us to be called his children—think of it—and we really *are!* But since most people don't know God, naturally they don't understand that we are his children.

2 Yes, dear friends, we are already God's children, right now, and we can't even imagine what it is going to be like later on. But we do know this, that when he comes we will be like him, as a result of seeing him as he really is.

GALATIANS 4

1 But remember this, that if a father dies and leaves great wealth for his little son, that child is not much better off than a slave until he grows up, even though he actually owns everything his father had.

2 He has to do what his guardians and managers tell him to, until he reaches whatever age his father set.

3 And that is the way it was with us before Christ came. We were slaves to Jewish laws and rituals for we thought they could save us.

4 But when the right time came, the time God decided on, he sent his Son, born of a woman, born as a Jew,

5 To buy freedom for us who were slaves to the law so that he could adopt us as his very own sons.

6 And because we are his sons God has sent the Spirit of his Son into our hearts, so now we can rightly speak of God as our dear Father.

7 Now we are no longer slaves, but God's own sons. And since we are his sons, everything he has belongs to us, for that is the way God planned.

God's great compassion, keep it in mind

ISAIAH 40

11 He will feed his flock like a shepherd; he will carry the lambs in his arms and gently lead the ewes with young.

ISAIAH 46

3b . . . I have created you and cared for you since you were born.
4 I will be your God through all your lifetime, yes, even when your hair is white with age. I made you and I will care for you. I will carry you along and be your Savior.

~26~

When You Feel Weak, Incapable

There is help

ZECHARIAH 4

6b . . . Not by might, nor by power, but by my Spirit, says the Lord of Hosts—you will succeed because of my Spirit, though you are few and weak.

PSALM 18

29 Now in your strength I can scale any wall, attack any troop.
30 What a God he is! How perfect in every way! All his promises prove true. He is a shield for everyone who hides behind him.
31 For who is God except our Lord? Who but he is as a rock?
32 He fills me with strength and protects me wherever I go.
33 He gives me the surefootedness of a mountain goat upon the crags. He leads me safely along the top of the cliffs.

PHILIPPIANS 4

13 For I can do everything God asks me to with the help of Christ who gives me the strength and power.

PSALM 94

16 Who will protect me from the wicked? Who will be my shield?

17 I would have died unless the Lord had helped me.

18 I screamed, "I'm slipping, Lord!" and he was kind and saved me.

19 Lord, when doubts fill my mind, when my heart is in turmoil, quiet me and give me renewed hope and cheer.

HEBREWS 13

6 That is why we can say without any doubt or fear, "The Lord is my Helper and I am not afraid of anything that mere man can do to me."

8 Jesus Christ is the same yesterday, today, and forever.

ISAIAH 40

28 Don't you yet understand? Don't you know by now that the everlasting God, the Creator of the farthest parts of the earth, never grows faint or weary? No one can fathom the depths of his understanding.

29 He gives power to the tired and worn out, and strength to the weak.

ZECHARIAH 10

12 The Lord says, "I will make my people strong with power from me! They will go wherever they wish, and wherever they go, they will be under my personal care."

2 CORINTHIANS 4

16 That is why we never give up. Though our bodies are dying, our inner strength in the Lord is growing every day.

PSALM 91

1 We live within the shadow of the Almighty, sheltered by the God who is above all gods.

2 This I declare, that he alone is my refuge, my place of safety; he is my God, and I am trusting him.

3 For he rescues you from every trap, and protects you from the fatal plague.

4 He will shield you with his wings! They will shelter you. His faithful promises are your armor.

5 Now you don't need to be afraid of the dark any more, nor fear the dangers of the day;

6 nor dread the plagues of darkness, nor disasters in the morning.

2 Corinthians 13

3b ... Christ is not weak in his dealings with you, but is a mighty power within you.

Ephesians 1

18 I pray that your hearts will be flooded with light so that you can see something of the future he has called you to share. I want you to realize that God has been made rich because we who are Christ's have been given to him!

19 I pray that you will begin to understand how incredibly great his power is to help those who believe him. It is that same mighty power

20 That raised Christ from the dead and seated him in the place of honor at God's right hand in heaven ...

2 Timothy 2

13 Even when we are too weak to have any faith left, he remains faithful to us and will help us, for he cannot disown us who are part of himself, and he will always carry out his promises to us.

Habakkuk 3

19 The Lord God is my Strength, and he will give me the speed of a deer and bring me safely over the mountains.

LUKE 18

27 He replied, "God can do what men can't!"

EPHESIANS 6

10 Last of all I want to remind you that your strength must come from the Lord's mighty power within you.

PSALM 89

7 The highest of angelic powers stand in dread and awe of him. Who is as revered as he by those surrounding him?

8 O Jehovah, Commander of the heavenly armies, where is there any other Mighty One like you? Faithfulness is your very character.

9 You rule the oceans when their waves arise in fearful storms; you speak, and they lie still.

11 The heavens are yours, the world, everything—for you created them all.

12 You created north and south! Mount Tabor and Mount Hermon rejoice to be signed by your name as their maker!

13 Strong is your arm! Strong is your hand! Your right hand is lifted high in glorious strength.

MARK 11

22,23 In reply Jesus said to the disciples, "If you only have faith in God—this is the absolute truth—you can say to this Mount of Olives, 'Rise up and fall into the Mediterranean,' and your command will be obeyed. All that's required is that you really believe and have no doubt!

24 Listen to me! You can pray for *anything*, and *if you believe, you have it;* it's yours!

25 But when you are praying, first forgive anyone you are holding a grudge against, so that your Father in heaven will forgive you your sins too."

JOSHUA 1

9 Yes, be bold and strong! Banish fear and doubt! For remember, the Lord your God is with you wherever you go.

EPHESIANS 3

20 Now glory be to God who by his mighty power at work within us is able to do far more than we would ever dare to ask or even dream of—infinitely beyond our highest prayers, desires, thoughts, or hopes.

21 May he be given glory forever and ever through endless ages because of his master plan of salvation for the church through Jesus Christ.

2 SAMUEL 22

29 O Lord, you are my light! You make my darkness bright!

30 By your power I can crush an army; by your strength I leap over a wall.

31 As for God, his way is perfect; the word of the Lord is true. He shields all who hide behind him.

32 Our Lord alone is God; we have no other Savior.

33 God is my strong fortress; he has made me safe.

34 He causes the good to walk a steady tread like mountain goats upon the rocks.

37 You have made wide steps for my feet, to keep them from slipping.

50 No wonder I give thanks to you, O Lord, among the nations; and sing praises to your name.

ROMANS 8

14 For all who are led by the Spirit of God are sons of God.

15 And so we should not be like cringing, fearful slaves, but we should behave like God's very own children, adopted into the bosom of his family, and calling to him, "Father, Father."

16 For his Holy Spirit speaks to us deep in our hearts, and tells us that we really are God's children.

HEBREWS 3

6 But Christ, God's faithful Son, is in complete charge of God's house. And we Christians are God's house—he lives in us!—if we keep up our courage firm to the end, and our joy and our trust in the Lord.

2 CHRONICLES 20

15b . . . The Lord says, "Don't be afraid! Don't be paralyzed by this mighty army! For the battle is not yours, but God's!"

In our weakness, we discover God's strength

2 CORINTHIANS 12

7 I will say this: because these experiences I had were so tremendous, God was afraid I might be puffed up by them; so I was given a physical condition which has been a thorn in my flesh, a messenger from Satan to hurt and bother me, and prick my pride.

8 Three different times I begged God to make me well again.

9 Each time he said, "No. But I am with you; that is all you need. My power shows up best in weak people." Now I am glad to boast about how weak I am; I am glad to be a living demonstration of Christ's power, instead of showing off my own power and abilities.

10 Since I know it is all for Christ's good, I am quite happy about "the thorn," and about insults and hardships, persecutions and difficulties; for when I am weak, then I am strong—the less I have, the more I depend on him.

2 CORINTHIANS 13

3 I will give you all the proof you want that Christ speaks through me. Christ is not weak in his dealings with you, but is a mighty power within you.

4 His weak, human body died on the cross, but now he lives by the mighty power of God. We, too, are weak in our bodies, as he was, but now we live and are strong, as he is, and have all of God's power to use in dealing with you.

5 Check up on yourselves. Are you really Christians? Do you pass the test? Do you feel Christ's presence and power more and more within you? Or are you just pretending to be Christians when actually you aren't at all?

~27~

When You Feel Worthless, Insignificant

Who is a worthless person?

PROVERBS 6

12,13 Let me describe for you a worthless and a wicked man; first, he is a constant liar; he signals his true intentions to his friends with eyes and feet and fingers.

14 Next, his heart is full of rebellion. And he spends his time thinking of all the evil he can do, and stirring up discontent.

15 But he will be destroyed suddenly, broken beyond hope of healing.

16-19 For there are six things the Lord hates—no, seven: haughtiness, lying, murdering, plotting evil, eagerness to do wrong, a false witness, sowing discord among brothers.

JEREMIAH 17

5 The Lord says: Cursed is the man who puts his trust in mortal man and turns his heart away from God.

6 He is like a stunted shrub in the desert, with no hope for the future; he lives on the salt-encrusted plains in the barren wilderness; good times pass him by forever.

What makes a person worthwhile?

1 SAMUEL 16

7 But the Lord said to Samuel, "Don't judge by a man's face or height, for this is not the one. I don't make decisions the way you do! Men judge by outward appearance, but I look at a man's thoughts and intentions."

JEREMIAH 17

7 But blessed is the man who trusts in the Lord and has made the Lord his hope and confidence.

8 He is like a tree planted along a riverbank, with its roots reaching deep into the water—a tree not bothered by the heat nor worried by long months of drought. Its leaves stay green and it goes right on producing all its luscious fruit.

LUKE 12

8 And I assure you of this: I, the Messiah, will publicly honor you in the presence of God's angels if you publicly acknowledge me here on earth as your Friend.

PROVERBS 18

12 Pride ends in destruction; humility ends in honor.

MATTHEW 23

11 The more lowly your service to others, the greater you are. To be the greatest, be a servant.

12 But those who think themselves great shall be disappointed and humbled; and those who humble themselves shall be exalted.

Luke 13

30 And note this: some who are despised now will be greatly honored then; and some who are highly thought of now will be least important then.

Luke 14

11 For everyone who tries to honor himself shall be humbled; and he who humbles himself shall be honored.

2 Corinthians 5

15 He died for all so that all who live—having received eternal life from him—might live no longer for themselves, to please themselves, but to spend their lives pleasing Christ who died and rose again for them.

16 So stop evaluating Christians by what the world thinks about them or by what they seem to be like on the outside.

2 Corinthians 2

14 But thanks be to God! For through what Christ has done, he has triumphed over us so that now wherever we go he uses us to tell others about the Lord and to spread the Gospel like a sweet perfume.

15 As far as God is concerned there is a sweet, wholesome fragrance in our lives. It is the fragrance of Christ within us, an aroma to both the saved and the unsaved all around us.

1 Corinthians 1

30 For it is from God alone that you have your life through Christ Jesus. He showed us God's plan of salvation; he was the one who made us acceptable to God; he made us pure and holy and gave himself to purchase our salvation.

When You Feel Worthless, Insignificant

ROMANS 8

1 So there is now no condemnation awaiting those who belong to Christ Jesus.

1 JOHN 1

9 But if we confess our sins to him, he can be depended on to forgive us and to cleanse us from every wrong. [And it is perfectly proper for God to do this for us because Christ died to wash away our sins.]

1 CORINTHIANS 13

1 If I had the gift of being able to speak in other languages without learning them, and could speak in every language there is in all of heaven and earth, but didn't love others, I would only be making noise.

2 If I had the gift of prophecy and knew all about what is going to happen in the future, knew everything about *everything*, but didn't love others, what good would it do? Even if I had the gift of faith so that I could speak to a mountain and make it move, I would still be worth nothing at all without love.

COLOSSIANS 3

9 Don't tell lies to each other; it was your old life with all its wickedness that did that sort of thing; now it is dead and gone.

10 You are living a brand new kind of life that is continually learning more and more of what is right, and trying constantly to be more and more like Christ who created this new life within you.

11 In this new life one's nationality or race or education or social position is unimportant; such things mean nothing. Whether a person has Christ is what matters, and he is equally available to all.

12 Since you have been chosen by God who has given you this new kind of life, and because of his deep love and concern for you, you should practice tenderhearted mercy and kindness to others.

Don't worry about making a good impression on them but be ready to suffer quietly and patiently.

13 Be gentle and ready to forgive; never hold grudges. Remember, the Lord forgave you, so you must forgive others.

JAMES 1

9 A Christian who doesn't amount to much in this world should be glad, for he is great in the Lord's sight.

10,11 But a rich man should be glad that his riches mean nothing to the Lord, for he will soon be gone, like a flower that has lost its beauty and fades away, withered—killed by the scorching summer sun.

PROVERBS 22

2 The rich and the poor are alike before the Lord who made them all.

How people in the Bible overcame feelings of inferiority

EXODUS 4

1 But Moses said, "They won't believe me! They won't do what *I* tell them to. They'll say, 'Jehovah never appeared to you!' "

10 But Moses pleaded, "O Lord, I'm just not a good speaker. I never have been, and I'm not now, even after you have spoken to me, for I have a speech impediment."

11 "Who makes mouths?" Jehovah asked him. "Isn't it I, the Lord? Who makes a man so that he can speak or not speak, see or not see, hear or not hear?

12 Now go ahead and do as I tell you, for I will help you to speak well, and I will tell you what to say."

13 But Moses said, "Lord, please! Send someone else."

14 Then the Lord became angry. "All right," he said, "your brother Aaron is a good speaker. And he is coming here to look for you, and will be very happy when he finds you.

15 So I will tell you what to tell him, and I will help both of you to speak well, and I will tell you what to do.

16 He will be your spokesman to the people. And you will be as God to him, telling him what to say ..."

JEREMIAH 1

4 The Lord said to me,

5 "I knew you before you were formed within your mother's womb; before you were born I sanctified you and appointed you as my spokesman to the world."

6 "O Lord God," I said, "I can't do that! I'm far too young! I'm only a youth!"

7 "Don't say that," he replied, "for you will go wherever I send you and speak whatever I tell you to.

8 And don't be afraid of the people, for I, the Lord, will be with you and see you through."

9 Then he touched my mouth and said, "See, I have put my words in your mouth!"

1 KINGS 3

7 O Lord my God, now you have made me the king instead of my father David, but I am as a little child who doesn't know his way around.

8 And here I am among your own chosen people, a nation so great that there are almost too many people to count!

9 Give me an understanding mind so that I can govern your people well and know the difference between what is right and what is wrong. For who by himself is able to carry such a heavy responsibility?"

10 The Lord was pleased with his reply and was glad that Solomon had asked for wisdom.

11 So he replied, "Because you have asked for wisdom in governing my people, and haven't asked for a long life or riches for yourself, or the defeat of your enemies—

12 Yes, I'll give you what you asked for! I will give you a wiser mind than anyone else has ever had or ever will have!

13 And I will also give you what you didn't ask for--riches and honor! And no one in all the world will be as rich and famous as you for the rest of your life!"

JAMES 4

5 Or what do you think the Scripture means when it says that the Holy Spirit, whom God has placed within us, watches over us with tender jealousy?

6 But he gives us more and more strength to stand against all such evil longings. As the Scripture says, God gives strength to the humble, but sets himself against the proud and haughty.

7 So give yourselves humbly to God. Resist the devil and he will flee from you.

8 And when you draw close to God, God will draw close to you. Wash your hands, you sinners, and let your hearts be filled with God alone to make them pure and true to him.

9 Let there be tears for the wrong things you have done. Let there be sorrow and sincere grief. Let there be sadness instead of laughter, and gloom instead of joy.

10 Then when you realize your worthlessness before the Lord, he will lift you up, encourage and help you.

Think about how God looks at Christians!

1 PETER 1

2 Dear friends, God the Father chose you long ago and knew you would become his children. And the Holy Spirit has been at work in your hearts, cleansing you with the blood of Jesus Christ and making you to please him. May God bless you richly and grant you increasing freedom from all anxiety and fear.

3 All honor to God, the God and Father of our Lord Jesus Christ; for it is his boundless mercy that has given us the privilege

of being born again, so that we are now members of God's own family.

JOHN 14

21 The one who obeys me is the one who loves me; and because he loves me, my Father will love him; and I will too, and I will reveal myself to him.

God gave you special abilities

1 CORINTHIANS 12

1 And now, brothers, I want to write about the special abilities the Holy Spirit gives to each of you, for I don't want any misunderstanding about them.

4 Now God gives us many kinds of special abilities, but it is the same Holy Spirit who is the source of them all.

5 There are different kinds of service to God, but it is the same Lord we are serving.

6 There are many ways in which God works in our lives, but it is the same God who does the work in and through all of us who are his.

7 The Holy Spirit displays God's power through each of us as a means of helping the entire church.

8 To one person the Spirit gives the ability to give wise advice; someone else may be especially good at studying and teaching, and this is his gift from the same Spirit.

9 He gives special faith to another, and to someone else the power to heal the sick.

10 He gives power for doing miracles to some, and to others power to prophesy and preach. He gives someone else the power to know whether evil spirits are speaking through those who claim to be giving God's messages—or whether it is really the Spirit of God who is speaking. Still another person is able to speak in languages he never learned; and others, who do not know the language either, are given power to understand what he is saying.

177

14 Yes, the body has many parts, not just one part.

15 If the foot says, "I am not a part of the body because I am not a hand," that does not make it any less a part of the body.

16 And what would you think if you heard an ear say, "I am not part of the body because I am only an ear, and not an eye"? Would that make it any less a part of the body?

17 Suppose the whole body were an eye—then how would you hear? Or if your whole body were just one big ear, how could you smell anything?

18 But that isn't the way God has made us. He has made many parts for our bodies and has put each part just where he wants it.

19 What a strange thing a body would be if it had only one part!

20 So he has made many parts, but still there is only one body.

21 The eye can never say to the hand, "I don't need you." The head can't say to the feet, "I don't need you."

22 And some of the parts that seem weakest and least important are really the most necessary.

23 Yes, we are especially glad to have some parts that seem rather odd! And we carefully protect from the eyes of others those parts that should not be seen,

24 while of course the parts that may be seen do not require this special care. So God has put the body together in such a way that extra honor and care are given to those parts that might otherwise seem less important.

25 This makes for happiness among the parts, so that the parts have the same care for each other that they do for themselves.

26 If one part suffers, all parts suffer with it, and if one part is honored, all the parts are glad.

27 Now here is what I am trying to say: All of you together are the one body of Christ and each one of you is a separate and necessary part of it.

ROMANS 12

3 As God's messenger I give each of you God's warning: Be honest in your estimate of yourselves, measuring your value by how much faith God has given you.

4,5 Just as there are many parts to our bodies, so it is with Christ's body. We are all parts of it, and it takes every one of us to make it complete, for we each have different work to do. So we belong to each other, and each needs all the others.

6 God has given each of us the ability to do certain things well.

Have You Heard of the Four Laws of Spiritual Life?

Four Laws of Spiritual Life

Just as there are physical laws that govern the physical universe, so are there spiritual laws which govern your relationship with God.

LAW ONE

God loves you and has a wonderful plan for your life.

God's love "For God so loved the world, that He gave His only begotten Son, that whoever believes in Him should not perish, but have eternal life" (John 3:16).

God's plan (Christ speaking): "I came that they might have life, and might have it abundantly" (that it might be full and meaningful) (John 10:10).

Why is it that most people are not experiencing the abundant life? **Because**

LAW TWO

Man is sinful and separated from God, thus he cannot know and experience God's love and plan for his life.

Man is sinful "For all have sinned and fall short of the glory of God" (Romans 3:23). Man was created to have fellowship with God; but because of his own stubborn self-will, he chose to go his own independent way and fellowship with God was broken. This self-will, characterized by an attitude of active rebellion or passive indifference, is an evidence of what the Bible calls sin.

Man is separated "For the wages of sin is death" (spiritual separation from God) (Romans 6:23). God is holy and man is sinful. A great chasm separates the two. Man is continually trying to reach God and the abundant life through his own efforts: good life, ethics, philosophy, etc.

The Third Law gives us the only answer to this dilemma . . .

LAW THREE

Jesus Christ is God's only provision for man's sin. Through Him you can know and experience God's love and plan for your life.

He died in our place "But God demonstrates His own love toward us, in that while we were yet sinners, Christ died for us" (Romans 5:8).

He rose from the dead "Christ died for our sins . . . He was buried . . . He was raised on the third day according to the Scriptures . . . He appeared to Cephas, then to the twelve. After that He appeared to more than five hundred . . ." (I Corinthians 15:3–6).

He is the only way "Jesus said to him, 'I am the way, and the truth, and the life; no one comes to the Father, but through Me' " (John 14:6). God has bridged the chasm which separates us from Him by sending His Son, Jesus Christ, to die on the cross in our place.

It is not enough just to know these three laws . . .

LAW FOUR

We must individually receive Jesus Christ as Savior and Lord; then we can know and experience God's love and plan for our lives.

We must receive Christ "But as many as received Him, to them He gave the right to become children of God, even to those who believe in His name" (John 1:12).

We receive Christ through faith "For by grace you have been saved through faith; and that not of yourselves, it is the gift of God; not as a result of works, that no one should boast" (Ephesians 2:8,9).

We receive Christ by personal invitation (Christ is speaking): "Behold, I stand at the door and knock; if any one hears My voice and opens the door, I will come in to him" (Revelation 3:20).

Receiving Christ involves turning to God from self, trusting Christ to come into our lives, to forgive our sins, and to make us what He wants us to be. It is not enough to give intellectual assent to His claims or to have an emotional experience.

These two circles represent two kinds of lives:

Self-controlled life

E—Ego or finite self on the throne

† —Christ outside the life

• —Interests controlled by self, often resulting in discord and frustration.

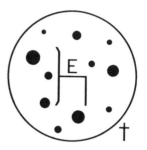

Christ-controlled life:

† —Christ on the throne of the life

E—Ego-self dethroned

• —Interests under control of infinite God, resulting in harmony with God's plan.

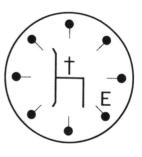

Which circle represents your life?

Which circle would you like to have represent your life?

The following explains how you can receive Christ:

YOU CAN RECEIVE CHRIST RIGHT NOW THROUGH PRAYER (PRAYER IS TALKING WITH GOD)

God knows your heart and is not so concerned with your words as He is with the attitude of your heart. The following is a suggested prayer:

"Lord Jesus, I need You. I open the door of my life and receive You as my Savior and Lord. Thank You for forgiving my sins. Take control of the throne of my life. Make me the kind of person You want me to be."

Does this prayer express the desire of your heart?

If it does, pray this prayer right now, and Christ will come into your life, as He promised.

HOW TO KNOW THAT CHRIST IS IN YOUR LIFE

Did you receive Christ into your life? According to His promise in Revelation 3:20, where is Christ right now in relation to you? Christ said that He would come into your life. Would He mislead you? On what authority do you know that God has answered your prayer? (The trustworthiness of God Himself and His Word.)

THE BIBLE PROMISES ETERNAL LIFE TO ALL WHO RECEIVE CHRIST

"And the witness is this, that God has given us eternal life, and this life is in His Son. He who has the Son has the life; he who does not have the Son of God does not have the life. These things I have written to you who believe in the name of the Son of God, in order that you may know that you have eternal life" (I John 5:11–13).

Thank God often that Christ is in your life and that He will never leave you (Hebrews 13:5). You can know that the living Christ indwells you, and that you have eternal life, from the very moment you invite Him in on the basis of His promise. He will not deceive you.

What about feelings?

DO NOT DEPEND UPON FEELINGS

The promise of God's Word, not our feelings, is our authority. The Christian lives by faith (trust) in the trustworthiness of God Himself and His Word. This train diagram illustrates the relationship between fact (God and His Word), faith (our trust in God and His

Word), and feeling (the result of our faith and obedience) (John 14:21).

The train will run with or without the caboose. However, it would be futile to attempt to pull the train by the caboose. In the same way, we, as Christians, do not depend on feelings or emotions, but place our faith (trust) in the trustworthiness of God and the promises of His Word.

NOW THAT YOU HAVE RECEIVED CHRIST

The moment that you, as an act of faith, received Christ, many things happened, including the following:
1. Christ came into your life (Revelation 3:20 and Colossians 1:27).
2. Your sins were forgiven (Colossians 1:14).
3. You became a child of God (John 1:12).
4. You began the great adventure for which God created you (John 10:10; II Corinthians 5:17 and I Thessalonians 5:18).

Can you think of anything more wonderful that could happen to you than receiving Christ? Would you like to thank God in prayer right now for what He has done for you? The very act of thanking God demonstrates faith.

Now what?

SUGGESTIONS FOR CHRISTIAN GROWTH

Spiritual growth results from trusting Jesus Christ. "The righteous man shall live by faith" (Galatians 3:11). A life of faith will enable you to trust God increasingly with every detail of your life, and to practice the following:

Have You Heard of the Four Laws of Spiritual Life?

G Go to God in prayer daily (John 15:7).

R Read God's Word daily (Acts 17:11)—begin with the Gospel of John.

O Obey God, moment by moment (John 14:21).

W Witness for Christ by your life and words (Matthew 4:19; John 15:8).

T Trust God for every detail of your life (I Peter 5:7).

H Holy Spirit—allow Him to control and empower your daily life and witness (Galatians 5:16,17; Acts 1:8).

THE IMPORTANCE OF A GOOD CHURCH

In Hebrews 10:25, we are admonished to forsake not "the assembling of ourselves together. . ." Several logs burn brightly together; but put one aside on the cold hearth and the fire goes out. So it is with your relationship to other Christians. If you do not belong to a church, do not wait to be invited. Take the initiative; call the pastor of a nearby church where Christ is honored and His Word is preached. Start this week, and make plans to attend regularly.